A PRACTICAL GUIDE TO RESUME PREPARATION AND JOB SEARCH

RESUME WRITING

MADE EASY

6TH EDITION

LOLA M. COXFORD

Prentice Hall
Upper Saddle River, New Jersey 07458

Library of Congress Cataloging-in-Publication Data

Coxford, Lola M.
    Resume writing made easy / Lola M. Coxford. -- 6th ed.
       p.   cm.
    Includes bibliographical references and index.
    ISBN 0-13-679853-5
    1. Résumés (Employment)   I. Title.
HF5383.C69   1998
650.14--dc21   97-22038
                            CIP

Acquisitions Editor: *Todd Rossell*
Managing Editor: *Mary Carnis*
Production: *Holcomb Hathaway, Inc.*
Production Liaison: *Adele Kupchik*
Director of Manufacturing and Production: *Bruce Johnson*
Manufacturing Buyer: *Marc Bove*
Marketing Manager: *Frank Mortimer, Jr.*
Cover Design: *Marianne Frasco*

 © 1998 by Prentice-Hall, Inc.
Simon & Schuster / A Viacom Company
Upper Saddle River, New Jersey 07458

Printed in the United States of America

10 9 8 7 6 5 4 3 2

ISBN 0-13-679853-5

Prentice-Hall International (UK) Limited, *London*
Prentice-Hall of Australia Pty. Limited, *Sydney*
Prentice-Hall Canada Inc., *Toronto*
Prentice-Hall Hispanoamericana, S.A., *Mexico*
Prentice-Hall of India Private Limited, *New Delhi*
Prentice-Hall of Japan, Inc., *Tokyo*
Simon & Schuster Asia Pte. Ltd., *Singapore*
Editora Prentice-Hall do Brasil, Ltda., *Rio de Janeiro*

CONTENTS

INDEX
OF RESUMES

Refer to the pages indicated for jobs or related jobs that appear in this guide.

HOW THIS BOOK CAN HELP YOU

The labor market has undergone many changes since the first edition of this book was published in the early 1980s. Some of these changes may already have affected you personally—perhaps you or a friend have been laid off at work, or perhaps you are a homemaker going to work outside the home for the first time. You may be a recent graduate of high school or college, looking for your first full-time job in a tough market. This book takes into account the changing times and the challenges of today's job market. It provides practical, effective advice for many different job seekers:

- Workers displaced due to company reorganization or downsizing
- Entry-level workers and liberal arts graduates having a difficult time in today's tight market
- Individuals returning to work outside the home with years of experience working inside the home
- Persons experiencing burnout in their present jobs
- Foreign-born applicants having difficulty convincing potential employers of their English proficiency
- Persons having to change career paths in order to navigate the changing labor market
- Individuals overcoming barriers encountered as a result of a physical disability
- Workers seeking to "move up" in their career field or explore a new or related field

Resume Writing Made Easy is a tool designed to help you get a job. People and their situations differ, but the basics of effective job search are universal, and the basic steps are all here:

- The resume
  —the various styles of resumes, including electronic resumes, and when each should be used
  —worksheets to record your skills, education, and experiences
  —lists of action and transition verbs to make your resume more dynamic
  —lots of sample resumes for you to study and adapt, broken into helpful categories: entry-level, transition, moving-up, and special needs
  —tips for bridging gaps between jobs or between education and work

—ideas for emphasizing your specific skills to match the employer's needs and to have those skills turn up in electronic searches

—guidelines for producing and reproducing a professional-looking, error-free resume

- The cover letter
  —how to personalize it
  —what to include
  —sample letters to study and adapt

- The job search
  —information interviewing
  —networking
  —exploring both the traditional and nontraditional job markets
  —sources of job information
  —keeping track of resumes sent, responses, and other important information
  —job hunting on the Internet

- The interview
  —sample questions that you can expect to be asked
  —advice on how to prepare for interview questions ahead of time so you won't be taken off guard
  —tips on how to dress and make a good first impression
  —how to follow up professionally (including a sample thank-you letter)

Combine your skill and diligence with the practical guidelines presented in this book to produce an attention-getting resume and thus take the first step toward the job you want. Good luck in your job search!

HOW TO USE THIS BOOK

Step 1 As any good coach will tell you, begin with the basics. Study Chapter 1 to learn how resumes are used, the different parts of a resume, and the several basic styles familiar to most personnel and recruiting people. You will then learn which style is best for you and which of the standard parts of a resume you should use when writing your own.

Step 2 Read Chapter 2 for a useful guide to your overall job search campaign. Learn about the hidden job market and learn how to network with others to increase your chances of finding a rewarding job that's right for you. Consider the suggestions regarding where to go to seek help with your job campaign. Finally, use the list of publications in Chapter 2 to research your areas of interest and look for job leads.

Step 3 In Chapter 3, fill out the Personal Inventory of information to have at hand when making up your resume. Learn how to use action verbs, skill verbs, and adjectives for describing your own personal traits. Study the many examples showing how to transpose your background and experiences into special skills. People who are hiring to fill vacancies are looking for skills and proven abilities, not just credentials or a list of your past jobs.

Step 4 Refer to Chapters 5 through 8 for specific information, suggestions, and sample resumes for four major groupings of job seekers. Chapter 5 concentrates on entry-level positions; Chapter 6 presents resumes for people "moving up"; Chapter 7 is for those displaced and in transition between careers; and Chapter 8 covers resumes for special purposes.

Step 5 Follow through in Chapter 4 by writing a rough draft: Pattern your resume after the suggested model and utilize information from the Personal Inventory you completed in Chapter 3 and the skills identified in the exercise following it. Experiment with different styles to determine which you like best. What works best will depend on your goals, your background, your tastes, and many other factors. Experiment, and then make a choice.

Step 6 Edit the rough draft in terms of fine points. Assume the role of the employer. Does this resume really *sell* you? If possible, have someone who is familiar with resumes, or at least a friend, review your rough draft and suggest possible improvements.

Step 7 Prepare the final copy. Refer to Chapter 4 for specifics on producing final copy and for suggested methods of duplicating the finished resume.

Step 8 In Chapter 9, note how cover letters are used, and examine the samples included.

Step 9 Refer to Chapter 10 for ways to keep track of and follow up on your efforts. This chapter includes sample thank-you and follow-up letters.

Step 10 Read Chapter 11 for tips on how to prepare for the interview. Study the section on "Questions Most Asked During an Interview," and write out your answers to the questions on the form provided.

Step 11 Learn in Chapter 12 what employers look for in a resume. Eight employers answer questions regarding what information they like to see in a resume, which formats they prefer, and other information.

By following these basic steps and using the techniques described here, you will be well on your way to a successful job search campaign. Good luck!

INFORMATION ABOUT RESUMES AND JOB SEARCH

WHY WRITE A RESUME?

Resumes continue to be one of the most important deciding factors in determining whether the job seeker gets an interview with the employer. A good resume gets a "foot in the door." Think of your resume as a sales tool. Just how well can you "sell" yourself? You are the product, and the employer is the buyer. Your resume must interest the employer in what you have to offer—namely, your skills, knowledge, and experience. Why should the employer invest time and money in you? What do you have to offer that is unique?

You may learn of an opening in a specific company through a friend, a classified ad, an agency, or on the Internet. Or you may wish to get an interview with a certain company without knowing whether they have any openings at this moment. In all these situations you need a good resume. Most employers are deluged with resumes. Resumes are used as screening devices to determine whom they are interested in interviewing.

A resume is a highly personal and individual summary of a person's background, experience, training, and skills. These factors will influence the final form of your own resume. Likewise, a good resume will vary depending on the type of job for which you are applying. Also, your own occupational group may be a factor requiring special consideration. For example, if you are a liberal arts graduate, you can direct your resume toward any number of areas. Your education has taught you how to communicate, lead others, be persuasive, solve problems, and plan. All of these are excellent skills for a management trainee position. The point is, you are selling your own unique combination of skills, and depending upon the job requirements, you should present your work experience, skills, and education to best reflect your qualifications for a particular job.

Preparing a good resume takes time. You should complete your resume before beginning your job search campaign. You will need a good resume to send to prospective employers and also to leave with those you contact when seeking information within a company. The contact person may be in a position to pass your resume along to someone who needs a person with your qualifications. If you are given an interview unexpectedly, a resume serves as a guide for the interviewer as well as an information source for you.

Every person, regardless of the present stage of his or her career, needs a good resume readily at hand. This is obvious if you are now actively seeking a job or a career change. Occasionally, however, you may need a current resume to capitalize on an unexpected job opportunity. Once you have worked up a good basic resume, you should be sure to keep it updated. It should always reflect your newly acquired skills and experience.

PARTS OF A RESUME

A resume must contain a certain amount of essential information. This information may vary from person to person depending on experience and qualifications. Categories that could be included are:

- Your name, address, city, state, and phone number(s) where you can be reached, and your e-mail address
- An objective statement that clearly describes the type of position you hope to obtain
- A summary of your qualifications
- A record of your employment history
- A record of your education
- Professional training
- Technological skills
- Professional affiliations
- A record of your military service if you consider it a "selling point" and particularly if your duties were job-related
- Licenses and accreditations
- Knowledge of foreign languages
- Publications
- Special accomplishments or other related facts
- A statement to the effect that your references and, if applicable, samples of your work, are available upon request

Few people will elect to use all these categories. When determining what information to include, consider what is relevant to the position for which you are applying. This selection is what will make your resume unique.

Name, Address, Telephone Numbers

Your name, address, city, state, and phone number(s) may seem too obvious to mention; however, this information has to be included, and it has to be correct. You should avoid the use of nicknames in a resume, and surnames such as "Junior," "Senior," "II," and "III" should be dropped. All words in the address should be spelled out (such as "Street," "Avenue," etc., and your state name), and the zip code included. The telephone number should be one where you can be reached easily. You may want to leave a brief message on your answering machine for added assurance.

The Career or Job Objective

Most resumes should include an objective statement of some type. This could be as simple as a one- or two-word description of the position you are seeking—staff accountant, computer programmer, nurse. Because the job objective is the "topic" of your resume, it should be the first and foremost consideration. The job objective says what you want to do, and it should say this as clearly and concisely as possible.

In any event, avoid the "all purpose" type of objective. You cannot sell a product successfully unless you are specific about its advantages to the buyer. Emphasize what you can do for the employer, not how you hope to benefit from the position. Be cautious about using overly ambitious statements such as, "Hope to advance to position of personnel manager." Your statement might be interpreted negatively and might be best left unsaid until the interview, when you have an opportunity for two-way communication.

If you have access to the exact job description, write your objective to match the employer's interests and needs.

Sample Career Objective Statements for Selected Positions

Accountant. Seeking an accounting position in an aggressive organization. Long-term plans are to advance into a major management responsibility within the financial function of the firm.

Biological Technician. Seeking an entry-level position in a biochemical laboratory, assisting biochemists in the chemical analysis of blood and other body fluids. Interested in working on environmental protection and control of air and water pollution.

Electronics Technician. Seeking a position in a medium-sized manufacturing company, testing, adjusting, and repairing electronic equipment.

Engineer. To obtain a position as an engineer in the field of structural engineering, stress analysis, or civil engineering.

Graphic Designer. To obtain a challenging full-time position in graphic design, specifically World Wide Web-based graphic design.

Health Care Administrator. Would like to provide high quality financial and human resources management services to a progressive organization in the health care industry.

Management. Management responsibility with an organization where demonstrated skills in sales, marketing, and administration can be translated into improved growth and profitability.

Marketing Assistant. A position as assistant in product marketing, development, or general research.

Office Manager. A challenging position as office manager that will give me an opportunity to use my established secretarial skills.

Personnel Assistant. A position as personnel assistant in the human resources department of a public service organization that would permit me an opportunity to utilize my knowledge of wage administration, grievance procedures, benefit programs publications, safety, labor relations, and employment.

Secretary. A position as executive secretary for a large sales organization.

Supervisor. A technical or supervisory position in which skills in quality control, management, and manufacturing would be an asset.

These are merely sample statements of objectives and goals you can use as a guideline in preparing your individual and unique objective statements. Your objective should reflect you. Try to make it comprehensive enough to be applicable to a number of employers, yet not so general that it is meaningless.

You will read other objective statements on the many sample resumes included in Chapters 5, 6, 7, and 8.

Summary of Qualifications

If your work experience has been varied and spread out over a number of years, consider the use of a Summary of Qualifications category. By providing a summary, you give the employer an overall picture of your qualifications before he or she reads further for details. This section allows creative job seekers to present their personal traits in a positive manner. One example of a Summary of Qualifications is:

> Have the ability to carry out programs under established policies and command the respect of staff. Problem solving, leadership, and communication skills are some of the qualities developed from my experience as an administrator, a supervisor, a teacher, and a customer relations representative.

Employment History

The employment history comes after the job objective and/or the Summary of Qualifications, unless you believe that education is your most qualifying feature for the job. This is often true for associate's, bachelor's, and master's degree candidates applying for entry-level positions. It is also true for the fields of teaching, engineering, law, and the like. Your educational background is generally less important the longer you are out of school.

Employment history can be listed in several ways, depending on the style of resume you choose (styles of resumes are discussed later in this chapter). If you elect to use the chronological format, list employment in reverse chronological order (your present or most recent job first). The important point is to emphasize that your skills and experience will be valuable to the employer. Most employers want dates of employment. Even if you use a functional or analytical resume, you should indicate length of experience. This does not necessarily mean using dates; for example, you could say "two years' experience selling. . . ."

The employment history section of your resume is the section that can be dealt with most creatively. Think of it as writing an advertising piece for yourself. This category allows you to create a dynamic resume that expresses the skills you possess. It should paint a portrait of yourself for the employer.

The total employment history should reflect your skills and make a positive impact on the employer. To achieve this, you must use action verbs and skill verbs. (More discussion of these verbs is found in Chapter 3.) In resumes, these two kinds of verbs are often used to begin sentences. Some examples of descriptions of past work experiences follow; the action verbs are underlined.

<u>Organized</u>, <u>computed</u>, and <u>maintained</u> confidential sales compensation records.

<u>Participated</u> <u>in</u> feasibility study and planning of computerized commission accounting system.

<u>Performed</u> all functions necessary for the preparation of manual and computer-processed payables.

<u>Developed</u> improved mailing system for company accounts.

<u>Reduced</u> manufacturing workforce by 15 percent while <u>exceeding</u> average production volume by more than 29 percent.

<u>Cut</u> the outage time of several important communications circuits in half, which resulted in a saving of over $22,000 over the two-year period.

Incorporate as many action verbs as possible (but don't go overboard). They are dynamic and forceful and tend to make an impression on the reader and portray you in a positive light. If you are having difficulty choosing the right word to describe your qualifications, experience, and accomplishments, the action and skill verbs listed in Chapter 3 may be helpful.

Study the list of personal traits, also in Chapter 3, for adjectives that best describe *you*. Keep these traits firmly planted in your mind as you write your descriptions; you should strive to convey that you are, for example, creative, logical, reliable, and so forth.

Education

The education section usually follows the employment history section unless you are recently out of school, in which case it precedes the employment history. If you have little or no practical experience, your academic credentials probably will be your strongest asset; in this case, place them directly after the objective statement. As you gain experience, your academic credentials become less important and usually are placed near the end of the resume. An exception to this rule is when the academic background is required for the job, as in the case of law or medicine.

Begin with your highest level of educational achievement. In this way, a doctorate will be followed by a master's degree, then a bachelor's. If you have not completed a college degree, list what you can. For example, if you have completed 25 units toward your associate of arts degree, state it, but do not add that you did not graduate. Rather, state that your objective is to work toward a higher degree, if that is the case. Drop reference to high school if you have attended college or have received some type of specialized training.

Degree, Diploma, or Certificate

Your evidence of having completed formal education is a degree, diploma, or certificate. This is not the place to be creative; list your degree as it was awarded by the institution. If you hold an A.A., B.S., M.A., M.S., or Ph.D., you can use abbreviations since everyone knows what they represent. For degrees that many people are not familiar with, such as B.F.A. (Bachelor of Fine Arts), it is better to spell out the degree.

Name of Institution

Give the name of the institution or organization where the learning occurred. Avoid abbreviations, and be certain to include the entire name (for example, University of Texas at El Paso).

Location of Institution

It is generally not necessary to include the city and state where your college is located if it is obvious from the name.

Date of Degree, Diploma, or Certificate

Include the date of degree, diploma, or certificate if you earned it in the last five years. If the degree is not recent, place the date at the end of the paragraph or omit it. You want to accent what you learned rather than when you learned it. This is especially true if you think your age might have a negative impact on the employer.

Major Area(s) of Study/GPA/Honors

You should include your major field of study if it applies directly to the job objective. If the major or minor field of study is not directly applicable, you may want to omit it to prevent your getting screened out by human resource professionals.

If you have an exceptionally high grade point average (3.5 or better), you may want to mention it. If you graduated with honors or if you graduated *Cum Laude* or *Summa Cum Laude*, you should include this information (use italic type or underlining with these titles, as shown here). For example:

B.S., *Cum Laude,* Mechanical Engineering Technology, New Jersey Institute of Technology, May 1994.

Finally, if you worked your way through college, state it. For example:

Earned 75 percent of college expenses.

Professional Training

It is generally best to separate education from training. Include this section when you wish to focus on special courses and seminars or other forms of continuing education. Seminars include those sponsored by your employer and those you have attended away from your place of employment. Training also includes college courses taken to improve your job performance. For example, this would be a good place to mention that you are computer literate and substantiate that claim with relevant coursework:

• Powerful Business Writing Skills, National Seminars, Inc. (8 hours) 1997

Technological Skills

A concise list of your technological skills, placed near the top of your resume, will be helpful to the employer. Include specific computer applications, programming languages, operating systems, and hardware, such as C++, Java, FileMaker, UNIX, Macintosh OS, Windows 95, and Imagesetter. Other technological skills include computer networking (local area networks and wide area networks), audio-video conferencing, video editing, Magnetic Resonance Imaging (MRI), and ultrasound technology.

Professional Affiliations

List only those memberships that directly relate to your career objective. By including associations and memberships you demonstrate that you are keeping up to date in your profession. For persons making a career change, a listing of professional memberships demonstrates that you are serious about your intent. Persons returning to work after an absence of years may want to take this opportunity to expand on any community involvement, such as PTA, Girl Scouts, Boy Scouts, and fundraising campaigns. Focus on involvements that demonstrate skills that would be useful in the position for which you are applying. For example:

> Chair, Culver City's 50th Birthday Celebration. Selected civic leaders as members of planning committee representing city hall, schools, businesses, and senior citizens. Organized dinner and entertainment arrangements for 500 people.

Military Service

Include this information if you feel it will be a selling point to the potential employer, particularly if your training and/or duties relate to the job for which you are applying. Provide branch of service, inclusive dates of service, and rank at time of discharge. Briefly state relevant duties and responsibilities, or simply state you received an honorable discharge.

Licenses and Accreditations

List only those credentials that are pertinent to the career objective; for example: possession of special teaching credentials or statements of having passed professional examinations such as the bar exam or CPA exam.

Foreign Languages

State any foreign languages you know, your level of proficiency, and any translating experiences you may have had.

Special Accomplishments

Career changers, recent college graduates, and women reentering the workforce can benefit from including a special accomplishments section. This section can also be labeled achievements, activities, projects, awards, volunteer experiences, or other related facts. For example:

- 1997 - Led sales force to a "win" in the "East vs. West" sales contest.
- 1996–1998, Big Brothers/Big Sisters volunteer.

References

Because most employers prefer to seek out their own sources for references, it is not necessary to devote space to listing them on a resume. Simply stating "References will be furnished upon request" should be sufficient.

WHAT NOT TO INCLUDE

Do not include your salary history or mention your salary requirements on the resume. Including such information is a lose–lose proposition. Naming a salary requirement that is too high may eliminate you from consideration; naming a low figure may indicate to employers that you will work for less than they otherwise would have offered. Wait until the interview stage to discuss salary requirements.

Leave out any reference to age, race, religion, sex, and national origin. Government legislation forbids discrimination in these areas and employers do not want to get involved in any legal problems. Omit any reference to your health and to your physical description unless your appearance is directly relevant to the job, such as an actor or model. Photographs have no place on the resume except for actors, models, or other entertainment personalities.

Remember, your resume sums up your accomplishments. Therefore, keep it as streamlined as possible. It is redundant to use a heading such as RESUME, FACT SHEET, or CURRICULUM VITAE. It is also unnecessary to say anything about your availability for employment or the reason you left your last job, as these are topics covered during the interview.

STYLES OF RESUMES

The three most widely used of the several basic resume styles are the chronological, functional, and combination. These three styles are extensively represented in this manual. A fourth style, the creative resume, specializes in selling creativity to the employer. A fifth style, the electronic resume, is an increasingly common style in this high-tech age.

The Chronological Resume

Because employers are interested in what you did and when you did it, the chronological resume has remained popular for some time. In this type of resume, you present your work experience and education in chronological order, beginning with the most recent. The chronological approach may be considered **most appropriate for people with two or more relevant job experiences.** It is less appropriate for recent graduates with little pertinent experience and for men and women returning to the workforce. It may not be appropriate for older people who are somewhat sensitive about their age, because it tends to emphasize dates. If experience is commensurate with age, however, there is no reason to hide the age.

The chronological resume is basically a record of work experiences including job descriptions. The chronological resume should include:

- Name, address, telephone number
- Working experience, in reverse chronological order (your present or last position first)
- Short description of each job and the dates of employment
- Educational background

Advantages

- Is easy to write
- Emphasizes career longevity
- Emphasizes growth and continuity in specific job categories

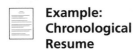

**Example:
Chronological
Resume**

FLORENCE GOLDBERG

3809 Miller Road, Lansing, Michigan 48910   (313) 344-6310

JOB OBJECTIVE: A challenging position as an Office Manager which will provide an opportunity to use my previous secretarial skills.

WORK EXPERIENCE:

1994–Present   Allied Supermarkets (Food Distributor) Detroit, Michigan

POSITION: **Keyline Artist - Advertising Department**

DUTIES: Created, set type for, and composed a four-page handbill. Also managed the advertising department in my boss's absence.

1988–1994   Allied Supermarkets (Food Distributor) Detroit, Michigan

POSITION: **Secretary - Advertising Department**

DUTIES: In addition to routine secretarial duties, worked directly with our customers. Ordered material for their stores and made sure they received their handbills on time. After doing this job for several years, was promoted to a keyline artist.

1985–1988   Murphy & Murphy, Inc. (Furniture Restorers) Detroit, Michigan

POSITION: **General Clerk**

DUTIES: Did the payroll, accounts receivable, accounts payable, and bank deposits. Also took orders from insurance agents.

EDUCATION:

Sept. 1996 to Present   I am working toward an A.A. degree at Lansing Community College, with a goal of transferring and obtaining a B.A. degree in Business Administration at Michigan State University, East Lansing.

Disadvantages

- Can be boring
- Makes it difficult to redirect your career
- Deemphasizes your transferable skills
- Enables detection of gaps in employment
- Emphasizes your most recent employment even if it is not the most important
- Can put older workers and perhaps younger workers at a disadvantage because it emphasizes dates

The Functional Resume

Many employers consider the functional resume the most useful type. The functional, or skills, resume allows you to be more flexible and creative in selling yourself to your prospective employer. The functional resume may be **useful if you have had limited work experience or if you have had a long break in your working experience.** It also is effective if you have been involved in volunteer work or cocurricular activities; this gives you an opportunity to bring out skills useful in a variety of working situations. Furthermore, this type of resume is used by professionals whose accumulated skills are more important than the chronological order of events in their work history. This style is especially effective for career redirection as it allows you to emphasize your strongest skills, talents, achievements, and capabilities. Individuals with unrelated work experience likewise should follow this format.

A functional resume is organized according to the functions of the job you wish to obtain. When you analyze your work history for a functional resume, you discover your own "hidden assets" and present them so they point directly to the position desired. You select only those facts from previous employment that relate to the job you are aiming for, and omit irrelevant experiences. For example, you may have screened phone calls, visitors, and correspondence on one job, prepared monthly reports on another, and maintained sales compensation records on a third. Experience in keeping records and preparing reports can be extremely useful in the field of personnel and related areas. In a functional resume this "hidden" organizational ability comes to light and is accented more than it is in any other style of resume.

Advantages

- Provides flexibility to emphasize strengths and areas of accomplishment
- Enables a prospective employer to place you in a position where your greatest assets can be utilized
- Allows you to be selective in the capabilities you want to use in your new career direction
- Eliminates the possibility of being placed in a position in which you no longer want to work
- Conceals gaps in your work history
- Allows you to examine your accomplishments in a positive manner and uncover "hidden" assets

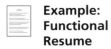 **Example:
Functional
Resume**

TREVOR S. HARDY
1611 Springdale Street
Atlanta, Georgia 30306
(404) 451-5340

OBJECTIVE

Personnel Management/Director

SUMMARY

Five years' personnel generalist/management experience, with specific emphasis on recruitment/employment of management, technical, and clerical personnel; employee/labor relations; E.E.O./A.A.; training; and wage/salary administration.

EXPERIENCE

- Solely responsible for recruitment, interviewing, hiring, and employee relations for 60 Southeastern restaurants while lowering turnover three years consecutively.
- Administered personnel and policies and practices, including affirmative action goals, while managing the regional unemployment insurance program; responded to and attended all labor relations hearings.
- Responsible for administering personnel, reserve, and regional office budgets totaling $195,000, arriving 11 percent under budget for fiscal year end.
- Developed and taught college courses in speech communications for Georgia State University, Atlanta.
- Other responsibilities include training and manpower development; management consulting for a wholly retained executive and professional search firm.

EMPLOYMENT

Southeastern Regional Personnel Manager
Restaurant Corporation, Atlanta, Georgia

Staff Associate
Wright Horton and Associates, Atlanta, Georgia

Lecturer P/T
Georgia State University, Atlanta, Georgia

EDUCATION

Georgia State University, Atlanta - 21 post-graduate units
Georgia State University, Atlanta - B.A. Speech Communication, 1990
Peachtree Community College, Atlanta - A.A. degree, 1986

Disadvantages

- Takes time and effort and is more difficult to write
- Employers may view negatively the omission of history

The Combination Resume

The combination resume can be considered **a cross between the functional and the chronological resumes.** This resume is similar to the functional resume except that company names and dates are included. The format allows an applicant to emphasize the preferred and most relevant skills, and at the same time it satisfies the employer's desire for names and dates.

The objective should be stated clearly in a sentence or two. You may wish to use a qualifications summary if you have had a variety of jobs or if your experience spans several years. In the "Experience" section give the name of the company, the location, and your position title. Describe in detail what your responsibilities were and, if possible, what happened as a result of your being there. Be sure to start the sentences with an active verb.

If you are applying for a position in sales management, for example, you could describe your ability to administer a program like this:

- Provided product specifications . . .
- Coordinated sales promotion . . .
- Completed service/sales training program . . .
- Evaluated sales campaign impact . . . .

The point stressed is your ability and accomplishments in terms that make you attractive to a potential employer.

As is the case with all three resume styles, the Education section begins with the highest degree first. Or, if you are in the process of obtaining a degree, give the date you expect to receive it and a list of major courses applicable to the objective. As with the two previously discussed styles, include other desirable information in categories listed as Special Accomplishments or Related Facts.

The Creative Resume

The creative resume is **more of a demonstration than a description of what you can do.** Some examples of careers for which this approach can be effective are:

- photographer
- musician
- advertising copywriter
- dancer
- technical writer
- graphic artist
- radio announcer
- model

For instance, a commercial artist might design a brochure that contains a resume and examples of her work to spark an employer's interest. Musicians and radio announcers could create audio tapes of their resumes as examples of their abilities, while a copywriter might incorporate his

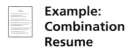

**Example:
Combination
Resume**

RICHARD L. DITTMAR
6168 Kentucky Drive
Buena Park, California 90621
(714) 992-5341

OBJECTIVE: A position using proven skills in all phases of programming. Special interest in computer control of external devices and artificial intelligence.

SPECIAL SKILLS

Programming
- Designed test fixture programs for diagnostic systems.
- Modified existing test fixtures and documented programs and modifications.
- Validated programs and modifications.
- Knowledgeable in the following computer languages: BASIC, PASCAL, C/C++, Fortran, and VP-Expert.

Hardware
- Constructed and conducted "final test" of completed diagnostic systems.

Communication
- Participated in design, validation, and team building meetings.
- Delivered several departmental presentations.

Artificial
Intelligence
- Trained in VP-Expert.
- Wrote personal programs using neural network theory.

EXPERIENCE

1989 to Present
- <u>Senior Electronic Technician</u>
  Fluor-Daniel, Inc. Irvine, CA

Write software for test fixtures, construct test fixtures, and rebuild and test returned systems. Complete "final test" of systems. Promoted from electronic technician to advanced electronic technician within the first three years.

EDUCATION

Working toward A.A. degree in Electronics Technical at Fullerton College, Irvine, CA. Have completed 46 units with a 4.00 average (4.00 scale). Major courses completed include: AC and DC Theory, Electrical Circuits and Systems, and Microcomputer Technology.

resume into ad copy. A photographer's resume might include a sample of her work or be accompanied by a set of slides, while a dancer might send a videotaped resume.

Examples of these types of resumes are difficult to show in a book. Remember to use this approach only if you work in a field where creativity is important and the medium (tape, videotape, etc.) is appropriate and showcases your skills. Also, be careful not to resort to gimmicks, as this can be a turn-off to employers. In most instances you would want to prepare a portfolio to be presented during the interview or as a follow-up. This style is not considered appropriate for most positions in business and industry. A more conservative style would be in keeping with the tradition prevalent in human resource departments.

The Electronic Resume

Submit your resume to a large company today, and chances are it will be electronically scanned into a computer database where employers can quickly search for candidates that match the company's needs. Your electronic resume, a slightly modified version of your traditional resume, will take advantage of this technology and improve your chances of obtaining an interview. It will also be suitable for distributing electronically, via the Internet.

The chief difference between the two resume formats is design. Since optical scanners are picky readers—they're not impressed by colored paper, fancy graphics and exotic typefaces—consider these guidelines:

- Print on 8 1/2 by 11-inch white copy grade (20-60 lb.) paper
- Use an easy-to-read typeface such as Helvetica, Times, or Palatino (approximately 12 points in size)
- Avoid underlines, boxes, columns, italics, and shading
- Use boldface type and bullets to emphasize words or phrases
- Limit resume to two separate pages
- Never fold an electronic resume

Employers search a database for key words such as "Internet proficient" and "MBA"; thus, your electronic resume should emphasize skills rather than achievements. This is the time to tout your Spanish fluency, knowledge of computer graphics software, and 90-words-per-minute typing speed!

A popular electronic resume format includes a brief skill summary at the top of the page, similar to the lead paragraph of a news article. A busy employer scrolling through dozens of resumes will immediately see your strongest skills and, if enticed, read further.

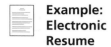
**Example:
Electronic
Resume**

SUSAN HALEY
842 West Tyler Avenue
Mill Valley, California 94941
415-380-5053   haley1@aol.com

OBJECTIVE: Public Relations Director

SKILL SUMMARY

Marketing, television production, fundraising, direction, writing, editing, public speaking, newsletter production and design, media relations, special events coordination, PageMaker, Microsoft Word, WordPerfect.

EXPERIENCE

Aldersly Retirement Community   San Rafael, CA
Director of Marketing   1997–Present

Responsible for all aspects of marketing, including public speaking engagements, senior health awareness workshops, fundraising, annual budgeting, and planned giving.

Severe Communications   Oklahoma City, OK
Public Relations, Marketing and Media Specialist   1993–1996

Created capital funds projects for numerous organizations. Produced and bought television, radio, and print advertising. Created public awareness campaigns and produced press releases. Responsible for overseeing new campaigns, newsletters, fund-raising, public relations projects, and budgeting consultation.

Canterbury Retirement Community   Oklahoma City, OK
Community Service/Resident Relations Director   1990–1993

Planned and implemented all social, cultural, and community events. Served as spokesperson and media relations coordinator.

EDUCATION

Oklahoma City University Business School
B.A., Business Administration/Public Relations

THE JOB SEARCH CAMPAIGN

STEPS IN THE PROCESS

Now that you have become familiar with the parts and styles of resumes, it is time to discuss resumes in the context of the job search process. As stated previously, the purpose of the resume is to *get the interview!* Therefore, you will want to do some research to decide how to focus your resume depending on the jobs for which you will be applying. Research will alert you to possible job opportunities and will help you to reach the decision makers in those companies. A job search campaign is really a campaign to market yourself, and the resume is only the beginning.

As a first step, determine a career objective. At times the first priority is simply to find a job to pay the rent, but even at those times, give some thought to choices and directions. If you are experiencing difficulties in making career goals, you may wish to seek the help of a professional career guidance counselor. Most community colleges now have career exploration courses and career resource centers where you can obtain guidance in formulating a plan.

Depending on your goals, you may find that the first step is to attain additional schooling or training. Consult your local community college, trade school, or vocational school for assistance in educational planning. For example, in today's competitive market you may find that computer proficiency is a basic requirement for many jobs.

The most important point to remember is that you do not have to perform your job search alone. Your community probably offers many resources, including counseling and job search education; local schools probably offer financial assistance; and temporary employment agencies can provide the means to work while going to school or continuing your job search.

A successful job search may take only weeks, or it can take several months. But, if you make use of all resources available to you, stay active, and keep making contacts, your chances of finding a good job are much improved.

PUBLISHED AND UNPUBLISHED JOB OPPORTUNITIES

The labor market can be divided into two parts. The first, the published part, consists of jobs advertised in the newspapers or online via your computer, those listed with college placement centers, and those available through employment agencies. Finding a job in this segment will require *traditional* strategies.

The second part, the unpublished part, is the much larger share of the job market. It is considered the "hidden" job market. For example, if you conduct a poll to determine how people located their present jobs, you will find that a majority of them heard about their jobs through an acquaintance, a relative, a friend, or a friend of a friend, or from leads they generated themselves through networking and research. Statistics indicate that 80 to 90 percent of all jobs are part of the hidden job market.

As you can see, it is extremely important that you begin making your own contacts. Finding a job in this market will require *nontraditional* strategies.

THE TRADITIONAL JOB SEARCH

You probably will want to use some traditional as well as nontraditional methods in your job search, to increase your chances of getting a job. Basically, the traditional job search sources are (a) employment agencies (or executive job search firms), (b) newspaper ads, (c) direct mail, (d) electronic databases, and (e) the Internet.

Employment Agencies and Executive Search Firms

One important source of job openings is an appropriate employment agency. Many agencies specialize in specific career areas such as accounting, bookkeeping, technical jobs, and so on. One way to find a good agency that is suitable to your job search is to call a few companies in which you would like to be employed and ask someone in the personnel or human resources department which employment agencies that organization uses.

An excellent intermediate step in the job search process is to use an agency for temporary employment while you are acquiring additional skills or continuing your job search process. Working part-time or even full-time on a temporary basis provides an excellent way to get out into the business world, make contacts, and do some job research of your own. This type of employment also can give you an "insider's edge" because many temporary employees are kept on permanently if they do an exceptional job and fit in with the organization.

You also might check with the personnel department of major firms to see if they have an internship program in their organization. More and more major employers are making use of temporary employees and interns as a cost-effective way of getting the job done.

If you are at a high management level, you may want to check out executive recruiters who are likely to have positions available in your field and at your level. Refer to the *Executive Employment Guide*, which lists more than 125 nationwide executive recruiters. (See the listing later in this chapter.)

Newspaper Ads

People still find jobs through newspaper want ads, so by all means include responses to classified ads as part of your job campaign. Remember, though, that only 15 to 20 percent of all available jobs appear in the want ads. Don't limit your job search to this strategy!

In general, most employment ads and services are listed in the classified sections of the Sunday local newspapers. But it is important to study daily newspapers to find their pattern for listing job opportunities. For instance, the *Wall Street Journal* features these ads every Tuesday, and the *Los Angeles Times* lists job opportunities daily in the classified section, with a heavier concentration on Sundays and special supplements periodically.

Be sure to look under all appropriate categories, and do it consistently. Some companies advertise by industry, others by function, still others by job title. For example, a job opening for a programmer might be found under the heading Computer Programmer, Data Processor, Application Programming, or simply Programmer. Some smaller newspapers may have no categories at all.

Another way to use the classified ads is to study them to see who is hiring, and for how much. Salary levels are now omitted from most ads, but occasionally you will find a salary range. This will give you an overall picture of the job market so you can assess which companies are consistently in need of employees. If you use this job search method be sure to keep accurate records and follow up on each application. (See Chapter 10 for ideas on how computer software programs can help manage this.)

In addition to employment ads, local job banks, job fairs, and other community resources are listed in the classified section. Take advantage of these opportunities whenever possible.

Direct Mail

You also may want to try your hand at advertising your skills through direct mail. With such campaigns the response is typically very low; however, you are much more likely to get replies if you have targeted an audience. Using the resources listed previously and in the rest of this chapter, target your resume and an appropriate cover letter to companies most likely to need your skills and qualifications. Limit your campaign to the geographical area in which you are interested. The Yellow Pages can also be a great help in locating companies in specific areas. Telephone directories for other locations can be found in your public library.

If you are an artistic, creative individual, you may want to devise a unique direct mail campaign appropriate to your field and expertise. For example, if you are seeking illustration or graphics work, your resume and your direct mail campaign should reflect your special talents. To target your campaign, spend time researching. One of the best places to start is in your local public or college library. Colleges also may have career centers with their own libraries. You may be surprised at the resources available to you.

Electronic Databases

While directories and periodicals can give you a wide range of information, there now are electronic versions of standard print publications. These electronic databases include a business directory that contains company reports as well as listings and mailing addresses of most companies whose stock is traded on the New York Stock Exchange. Among the features available are access to information by company name, zip code, area code, or by top sales for a specific time period. This information can be used in the library, or it can be downloaded to your own personal computer. These databases are now available at some of the larger public libraries. Contact your local library for further information.

College and university career development centers also may have created their own employer files or they may subscribe to the federal job listing and localized databases. One such database is the *Los Angeles Times National*, which lists the top 1,000 companies in California. Check with your local college or university career development center for further assistance with this valuable information.

The Internet

Every thorough job search should include a visit to "cyberspace." In fact, you might want to start there. With scores of resume databases, newspaper classified ads, and links to many major U. S. companies, the Internet—particularly its graphical interface, the World Wide Web—is a convenient and ever-growing job-hunting source. Finally, new online bulletin boards allow you to place messages to other job hunters, search for openings, post resumes, and make important contacts.

Using one of the many search tools available on the Web, such as Yahoo (http://www.yahoo.com), type "job" or "career." You will see a list of job databases and resume services from which to choose. Most of the services allow you to scan job listings and post your own resume to a database. Also, you may wish to read resumes posted by others in your field. Popular job databases include Career Mosaic (http://www.careermosaic.com), America's Help Wanted (http://www.jobquest.com) and Monster Board (http://www.monster.com).

(Caution: When posting your resume to a database, be aware of text formatting! Too many resumes on the Internet are difficult to read because of choppy-looking paragraphs or, even worse, sentences that drift endlessly off the screen. Follow the formatting instructions of the database, and check your resume once it has been posted.)

If you are targeting a particular company in your job search, look for its home page on the Web. Many companies post their job openings and allow you to submit your resume. While you're there, you might have access to company news and other information that would be helpful in writing a cover letter or preparing for an interview.

Another benefit of cyberspace: You can avoid newsprint-stained fingers by reading classified ads online. Major newspapers such as the *Los Angeles Times*, *The New York Times*, *The Boston Globe* and *Chicago Tribune* place their classified ads, in addition to their editorial content, on the Internet. See CareerPath (http://www.careerpath.com).

Finally, join a job-related Internet newsgroup where participants network, share strategies and swap resumes. Lively newsgroups include alt.jobs.offered and ba.jobs.offered. Additional career resources can be found on any of the major online companies, such as America Online and CompuServe.

THE NON-TRADITIONAL JOB SEARCH

The best way to find out about a job and to get a job is through contacts with *other people*. Numerous studies have confirmed this, and job search experts verify this as the most effective means of getting a job. The two primary ways of obtaining information about jobs are informational interviewing and networking.

Informational Interviewing

Your goal is to interview people who do the work you would like to do, who manage people who do that work, or who can offer you guidance or advice in your job search. These people will give you information about the job and the company that will help you determine whether the job is appropriate for you. In addition, making contact with these people may lead you to the person who does the hiring for such a position.

First of all, decide whom you would like to interview. Be sure to research the company before you talk to your contact so you will appear knowledgeable. Most people enjoy talking about themselves and their work, so this will help to put you at ease. At this time you are not asking for an employment interview; you are only seeking information. Some possible sources for contacts include:

- Former teachers or professors
- Civic leaders
- People in business (bankers, stockbrokers, real estate brokers, salespeople, and so on)
- Professionals (lawyers, executives, and so on)
- Clergy
- Co-workers and supervisors
- Friends, relatives, acquaintances

Most secretaries are trained to screen their employer's calls. Therefore, you will have to use special techniques to get to talk to the appropriate individual. Don't lie, but do try to avoid being turned away. Consider the following example:

Secretary:	May I tell him who is calling?
John Jones:	Yes, it's John Jones.
Secretary:	What is the nature of the call?
John Jones:	I'm doing research on your company and believe that Mr. Smith would be best prepared to answer the questions. Does he have a moment?
	Or: I'm writing a paper on advertising and would like to have permission to use ABC Company as an example.
	Or: I have a technical question concerning your company that I feel only Mr. Smith can answer. May I speak to him for just a minute, please?

Depending on your situation, you can use similar inquiries. The point is that you are doing research; you are striving to uncover information and trying, indirectly, to sell yourself to this individual. You may be making contact with someone who will later receive a resume from you and remember you favorably. You may be interviewing someone who could recommend you to an employer. These conversations may lead directly to an employment interview—but do not count that as the only satisfactory result. And do not push the possibility of an employment interview on someone who has been generous with his or her time and information.

Just as a salesperson expects to experience some rejection, you too will have to be prepared for that possibility. But the odds are still in your favor that you will be able to talk to someone. Best of all, you are in control of your job search.

Just what type of information should you be gathering from your contacts? Consider the following questions:

- Why did you decide to go into this field, and what academic preparation did you have?
- What do you like best about your position? Least?
- What personal qualities do you think are important in your work?
- Please describe the tasks you accomplish in a typical work day.
- If you were to give someone a word of advice about getting into this field, what would you say?
- What are the prospects for someone entering this field today?
- What advice would you give me for locating and obtaining a job in this field?
- Can you supply me with the names of three other persons who might be able to tell me more about this field?

After the interview ask yourself the following questions:

- Does this person use the skills I want to use?
- Would I be qualified for this job or for an entry-level job that will lead to a similar position?
- Do I understand what this job and this career entails?
- Would I enjoy working in this capacity?
- How can I follow up on any leads or ideas I received, or make additional contacts?
- What positive impression do I now have about this area of work?
- Have I left a positive impression with this individual in the event he or she plays a part in my continuing career search?

Networking

Networking refers to the *process of developing contacts and leads*. Networking was involved in the information interviewing just described, but there are other means of making contacts. The goal is to let people know you're looking for a job, to make a favorable impression on people you make contact with, and to be alert for leads and information. Most important, you must keep making contacts and follow up on all leads. If cultivated, contacts often make the difference between your being selected for a position and being overlooked.

Because advertising costs money and most employers realize that a good job will be filled quickly, many employers rely upon their present employees to refer qualified applicants for vacancies. Some companies go so far as to offer bonuses to employees who refer successful candidates. The typical employer feels more secure about an applicant referred by someone he or she knows than an individual recruited from a newspaper ad or from an agency. In addition, some jobs have to be filled before there is time to advertise.

Often people working in a given company will hear of job openings before the jobs are advertised or listed with employment agencies. If you hear about a job opening or believe one is about to occur, use your contacts to find out who knows somebody in power. Don't hesitate to ask a friend to introduce you to the proper person.

Networking is useful for individuals at all levels of employment. University alumni groups, fraternal organizations, and professional organizations are great networking resources. Your chosen field may have professional groups of which you are unaware. Use your local library to research local groups and attend meetings when appropriate. Contacts made in these groups can be of great value. In recent years women have begun making great use of networking and have set up organizations designed specifically for that purpose.

Some newspapers devote a special section to events and meetings. Consult your local newspaper for times and dates of meetings that you believe would allow you to network. For example, a local hotel may be having a convention that will involve exhibitors of products connected with your field of interest. At these gatherings you are likely to talk to people who share your interests and concerns. From these preliminary meetings you will gather information that will assist you in presenting your skills to a prospective employer in the best possible light.

After you have a firm grasp of what you want and how to target your job search efforts, the next chapters will help you refine your resume.

SOURCES OF INFORMATION

America's Corporate Families and *America's Corporate Families & International Affiliates.* (Three Volumes). Published annually by Dun & Bradstreet Corporation, 899 Eaton Avenue, Bethlehem, PA 18025–0001. Links parent companies with subsidiaries. Criteria for inclusion: two or more locations; 250+ employees, or $25 million sales volume, or tangible net worth greater than $500,000; controlling interest in one or more subsidiaries. Entries are arranged alphabetically by parent company, followed by subsidiaries arranged hierarchically. Cross-referenced by company names, geographical location, and SIC code.

College Placement Annual. Published annually by the College Placement Council, Inc., Box 2263, Bethlehem, Pennsylvania 18001. Contains information on firms and governmental agencies relating to occupational opportunities.

Contacts Unlimited. Published annually at 516 S. E. Morrison, Portland, Oregon 97214. Complete catalog of firms and personnel of a specific geographical location; listings by firm name, type of business, zip code area, name of key executives, and numerically by telephone number; contains a market planning section; includes monthly updates.

Dictionary of Occupational Titles (D.O.T.). Published by the Government Printing Office, Washington, D.C. 20402. Lists more than 35,000 job titles and more than 20,000 different occupations. An updated version was published in 1991.

Directory of Corporate Affiliations. (Five Volumes). Published annually by National Register Publishing, a Reed Reference Publishing Company, 121 Chanlon Road, New Providence, NJ 07974. The 110,000 entries include the most influential U. S. and foreign parent companies, both public and private, and all subsidiaries. Subsidiaries are listed in order of reporting hierarchy.

Dun's Directory of Service Companies. Published annually by Dun & Bradstreet Corporation, 899 Eaton Avenue, Bethlehem, PA 18025-0001. The 50,000 largest U. S. public and private companies in the service sector are listed alphabetically and geographically by industry (SIC).

Directory of Executive Recruiters. Published by Consultants News, Fitzwilliam, New Hampshire 03447 (1986). Information on 1,479 executive search firms in the United States, Canada, and Mexico. Offers tips on how to work with recruiters and what to look for in a search firm.

Encyclopedia of Associations. Published by Gale Research Company, Book Tower, Detroit, Michigan 48226. A guide to national and international nonprofit organizations; includes information on location, size, and objectives of more than 14,500 trade associations, professional societies, labor unions, and fraternal and patriotic organizations.

Executive Employment Guide. Published by the American Management Association, 135 West 50th Street, New York, New York 10020. Contains a list of more than 125 nationwide executive recruiters including addresses, phone numbers, fields covered, minimum salaries of positions handled, and an indication as to whether each accepts resumes or will be willing to set up an interview.

Guide to Occupational Exploration. Published by the U.S. Government Printing Office, Washington, D.C. 20402. Data are organized into 12 interest areas, 66 worker trait groups, and 348 sub-groupings.

Hoover's Handbook of American Companies. Published annually by Reference Press, Inc., 6448 Highway 290 East, Austin, TX 78723. Contains profiles of 500 selected major U.S. companies, public and private; includes a section of lists including the *Fortune 500* largest employers.

Literary Market Place. Published annually by the Directory of American Book Publishing, R. R. Bowker Company, 1180 Avenue of the Americas, New York, New York 10036. Includes lists of book publishers and types of books they publish, agents and agencies, wholesalers, exporters and importers, magazine and newspaper publishers; includes listings of services and suppliers to the book publishing industry.

Martindale-Hubbell Law Directory. Published annually at 1 Prospect Street, Summit, New Jersey 07901. Complete legal directory in seven volumes; includes listing of law firms in the United States, their staff, and biographical sketches of personnel.

Million Dollar Directory. (Five Volumes). Published annually by Dun & Bradstreet Corporation, 899 Eaton Avenue, Bethlehem, PA 18025–0001. Lists the top 160,000 U. S. public and private companies. Criteria for inclusion: headquarters or single location and 250+ employees, or $25 million annual sales volume, or net worth greater than $500,000. Volumes I–III, alphabetical listing of companies; Volume IV, companies are cross-referenced by industry; Volume V, companies are cross-referenced by geography.

Moody's Industrial Manual, Volumes I and II. Published annually by Moody's Investors Service, a company of the Dun and Bradstreet Corporation, 99 Church Street, New York, New York 10007. Covers companies listed on the New York and American Stock Exchanges as well as companies listed on regional American exchanges. Includes history of the company, products, names of officers and directors, capital structure, and financial statements.

National Trade and Professional Associations and Labor Unions of the United States and Canada. Published annually by Columbia Books, Inc., 777-14th Street NW, Washington D.C. 20005. Listing of more than 6,300 trade associations; labor unions; professional, scientific, or technical societies; and other national organizations composed of groups united for a common purpose; includes membership, annual budget, and publications.

Occupational Outlook Handbook. Published annually by the U.S. Government Printing Office, Washington, D.C. 20402. Includes information on job descriptions, places of employment, training, educational requirements, and salary ranges.

Peterson's Annual Guide to Careers and Employment (for Engineers, Computer Scientists, and Physical Scientists). Published annually by Peterson's Guides, P.O. Box 2123, Princeton, New Jersey 08540. Describes entry-level opportunities for technical bachelor's, master's, and doctoral degree holders including salary ranges, starting assignments, training programs, summer and co-op programs, international placements; includes information for mid-career professionals; covers nearly 1,000 companies hiring technical graduates.

Principal International Business. Published annually by Dun & Bradstreet Corporation, 899 Eaton Avenue, Bethlehem, PA 18025–0001. Lists 55,000 businesses in 143 countries worldwide chosen for size, prominence, and international interest; arranged by country, cross-referenced by company name and by product classification.

Standard & Poor's Register of Corporations, Directors and Executives. Published annually at 25 Broadway, New York, New York 10004. Contains alphabetical list showing business affiliations, business addresses, and residence addresses of individuals serving as officers, directors, trustees, partners, and similar roles in business and professional organizations.

Standard Directory of Advertising Agencies and Standard Directory of Advertisers. Published by the National Register Publishing Company, 5201 Old Orchard Road, Skokie, Illinois 60076. Includes alphabetical and trade name indexes; a guide to 17,000 corporations.

Thomas Register of American Manufacturers. Published annually by Thomas Register Publishing Company, 1 Penn Plaza, New York, New York 10001. In-depth information on products and services, company location, divisions, subsidiaries, and sales offices; includes products and services volumes, company volumes, and catalog volumes.

Who Owns Whom. (Four Volumes). Published annually by Dun & Bradstreet Corporation, 899 Eaton Avenue, Bethlehem, PA 18025–0001. Attempts to cover all corporate groups worldwide, public and private, regardless of size. Each volume covers a geographical area of the world. Arrangement is alphabetical by parent company, followed by hierarchical listing of subsidiaries, wherever located; includes indexes of subsidiaries, foreign parents, company name, and product classification.

3 LAYING THE GROUNDWORK FOR YOUR RESUME

MATCHING YOUR SKILLS TO THE JOB SPECIFICATION

Employers are always interested in potential job performance. In considering your resume, they will be concerned with what skills, in the broad sense of the word, you can bring to a position. Your skills can be divided into three categories:

1. Functional or transferable
2. Adaptive or personal
3. Technical

Each category is potentially valuable for your resume, and a complete listing of your skills will give you perspective on their value to you.

Functional (Transferable) Skills

Functional skills are those you can take with you from job to job. Some examples are:

organizing, problem solving, leading, persuading, negotiating, coordinating.

The following list suggests a variety of action and skill verbs that demonstrate functional skills you may wish to include in your resume.

Action Verbs

accelerated	attained	conserved
accomplished	blended	constructed
achieved	brought	consulted
acquired	built	contracted
acted	calculated	controlled
adapted	carried out	cooperated
administered	cataloged	coordinated
advanced	changed	corrected
advised	charted	counseled
allocated	classified	created
analyzed	collaborated	dealt
applied	collected	decided
approved	compared	decreased
arbitrated	completed	defined
arranged	computed	delegated
assembled	conceived	delivered
assisted	conducted	derived

designated
designed
detected
determined
developed
devised
diagnosed
directed
discovered
distributed
documented
doubled
drafted
edited
eliminated
encouraged
engineered
enlarged
escalated
established
estimated
evaluated
examined
expanded
experienced
explored
facilitated
finalized
formulated
founded
functioned
governed
grouped
guided
handled
harmonized
harnessed
headed
identified
implemented
improved
increased
indexed
initiated
inspected
installed
instituted
instructed
interpreted
interviewed
introduced
invented
investigated

justified
launched
led
localized
located
logged
made
maintained
managed
mastered
mechanized
merged
moderated
monitored
motivated
negotiated
obtained
opened
operated
ordered
organized
originated
overcame
perceived
performed
pioneered
planned
prepared
prescribed
presented
presided
processed
produced
programmed
promoted
protected
provided
purchased
quadrupled
raised
realized
received
recommended
recorded
recruited
rectified
redesigned
reduced
reevaluated
referred
reorganized
repaired
replaced

represented
reshaped
restored
resulting in
reversed
reviewed
revised
saved
scheduled
screened
selected
serviced
set up
sold
solved
sorted
sparked
specified
standardized
started
stimulated
straightened
strategized
streamlined
strengthened
succeeded in
summarized
supervised
supplied
supported
surpassed
systematized
tested
trained
transacted
transcended
transcribed
transformed
translated
trimmed
tripled
underwrote
unified
unraveled
upgraded
validated
varied
verified
vitalized
won
worked
wrote

Adaptive or Personal Skills

Adaptive skills or personal traits may best be defined as those that describe you. Some examples are:

creative, dependable, efficient, innovative, competent.

The following list suggests adaptive skills or traits that you may want to consider including in your resume:

Personal Traits

accurate	experienced	pleasant
active	fair	positive
adaptable	firm	practical
adept	genuine	productive
broad-minded	honest	reliable
competent	innovative	resourceful
conscientious	instrumental	self-disciplined
creative	logical	self-reliant
dependable	loyal	sense of humor
determined	mature	sensitive
diplomatic	methodical	sincere
discreet	motivated	successful
efficient	objective	tactful
energetic	outgoing	trustworthy
enterprising	participative	
enthusiastic	personable	

Technical Skills

A person acquires technical skills through learning and experience. They may or may not be transferable. Some examples of technical skills are:

typing, filing, drafting, welding, technical writing, accounting.

Obviously, the list of technical skills you might have acquired covers too wide a range to list here, but you should carefully review your experiences and list completely those skills you can perform. They provide a strong selling point for you to your prospective employer.

Determining Your Skills

How do you know what skills you have to offer an employer? The following exercise will help you identify your skills by having you recollect what you actually did in your past work experiences. Complete the following exercise for one or more of your past jobs. (If you are just entering the job force, list skills you have developed in school, in volunteer work, in household management, and so on. Also, see the discussion "Situations That Call for Special Techniques" on pp. 35).

Skills Identification

Title of Position: _____

Step One

Describe in detail what you did on this job during an average day, week, and month. Include specific responsibilities, number of persons supervised, budgets controlled, programs managed, sales generated, and so on.

_____

_____

_____

_____

_____

_____

_____

_____

Step Two

Describe skills, abilities, and talents demonstrated in carrying out your duties; for example: abilities to solve problems, achieve goals, introduce innovative techniques, reduce costs, increase efficiency; leadership qualities; abilities in planning, staffing, organizing, and controlling; human relations skills; and so on.

_____

_____

_____

_____

_____

_____

_____

_____

Step Three

Now go back and analyze the various entries you made in Step Two. What attributes, abilities, or skills show up most frequently? You will begin to see your own talents, your individual way of performing the job. Select three or four skills that are repeated most, and list them. You may wish to highlight these skills in the left margin of your resume. (Several sample resumes in this manual illustrate the technique.)

_____

_____

_____

_____

_____

_____

_____

_____

Step Four

Refer to the employer's job specification (if one is available), and pick out from your list of accomplishments those that you think most clearly fit the job. This is probably the most important key to a successful resume: matching your skills to that of the job specification. If it is not possible to obtain a printed job specification, talk to the person who has the power to hire or to someone close to that capacity to determine exactly what the employer is looking for. Try to get the person to be as specific as possible, and ask for details.

If you are transferring skills from a volunteer experience, consider the following example:

Volunteer Experience	Tasks and Responsibilities	General Skills, Qualities, and Traits
Organizing and chairing an art auction as a fund raiser for a women's organization	Contact artists to participate Decide amount of space needed Determine equipment needed (tables, lights, etc.) Decide on location for the event Determine rental fee for booths and entrance fee Determine costs for food, materials Solicit volunteers from membership Determine committee chairpersons and tasks Contact newspapers, printers, and art associations for publicity Plan publicity strategy	Develop conceptual plan for project Communicate with business community Schedule events and people Formulate policies, procedures, budgets Design, coordinate physical layout Supervise, select people, and delegate tasks Establish and maintain good interpersonal relationships with volunteers, business Write copy for ads, make oral presentations for publicity Motivate personnel, volunteers to support activity

PERSONAL INVENTORY

The most successful job seekers are those who do the necessary homework beforehand. This homework involves taking inventory of yourself. The Personal Inventory that follows has been designed to assist you in recollecting past experiences. Take sufficient time to fill it out. You will want to refer to the completed inventory when you are ready to begin your rough draft of the resume. This Personal Inventory is organized into categories that generally correspond to those listed in "Parts of the Resume." By carefully filling in this Personal Inventory, you will be organizing your own resume information in preparation for the first rough draft of the resume. Spaces are provided to list three jobs; begin with your most recent work experience.

Personal Inventory

Name _____

Address _____

_____
(City)   (State)   (Zip Code)

Telephone (Home) (____) _____ (Office) (____) _____ Email: _____

Skills/Qualifications Summary _____

_____

Work Experience (Full- and Part-time)

Job Title _____

Company, Agency, or Institution _____

Type of Business (If not clear from name) _____

Skills/Qualifications _____

Division or Department _____

Company Location _____

Dates of Employment _____
                          (From)   (To)

Major Responsibilities _____

_____

_____

_____

_____

Major Accomplishments, Contributions, Achievements _____

_____

_____

_____

_____

_____

Number of Persons Supervised _____

Work Experience (Full- and Part-time)

Job Title _____

Company, Agency, or Institution _____

Type of Business (If not clear from name) _____

Skills/Qualifications _____

Division or Department _____

Company Location _____

Dates of Employment _____
                    (From)   (To)

Major Responsibilities _____

_____

_____

_____

_____

Major Accomplishments, Contributions, Achievements _____

_____

_____

_____

_____

_____

Number of Persons Supervised _____

Work Experience (Full- and Part-time)

Job Title _____

Company, Agency, or Institution _____

Type of Business (If not clear from name) _____

Skills/Qualifications _____

Division or Department _____

Company Location _____

Dates of Employment _____
                    (From)   (To)

Major Responsibilities _____

_____

_____

_____

_____

Major Accomplishments, Contributions, Achievements _____

_____

_____

_____

_____

_____

Number of Persons Supervised _____

Unpaid Work Experience (Volunteer work, internships, work study, etc.)

_____

_____

_____

_____

_____

Education

(List all degree and certificate programs, and special courses taken at educational institutions.)

Degree or Certificate _____

Major or Course Emphasis _____

Minor _____

School Name _____

Dates of Education _____
                             (From)   (To)

Courses Relevant to Career Objective _____

_____

_____

_____

Overall Grade Point Average (Optional) _____

Special Projects or Presentations (Applicable to Objective) _____

_____

_____

_____

Professional Training

Workshop or Seminar _____

_____

Company Name _____

Dates of Training _____
                             (From)   (To)

Memberships

(List job-related professional or civic organizations that you belong to and participated with.)

Name _____

Type of Organization _____

Responsibilities and Accomplishments _____

Military

Branch of Service _____ Attained Rank _____

Length of Service (Inclusive dates) _____

Training Received _____

_____

_____

Major Responsibilities _____

Major Accomplishments, Contributions, Achievements _____

_____

_____

_____

Special Recognition

(List any awards, honors, or professional recognition you may have received.)

_____

_____

_____

_____

_____

_____

Special Accomplishments

(List publications, foreign language ability, special licenses, or talents such as music, art, drama.)

_____

_____

_____

_____

_____

_____

_____

SITUATIONS CALLING FOR SPECIAL TECHNIQUES

Not everyone has work experience and education that fits into what employers may refer to as the "ideal" package. For that reason, this book stresses special techniques to be used by those who lack some of the qualifications necessary to be competitive in today's labor market. The following guidelines apply to various situations.

Limited Formal Education

1. Sell work experience and on-the-job accomplishments.
2. Sell the education you do have, such as selected courses, seminars, workshops, conferences, military and company-related training.
3. Sell volunteer experience and emphasize accomplishments.

Formal Education in Different Field

1. Sell your work experience and transferable skills.
2. Slant the educational achievements you have for the job you want.
3. Indicate desire to pursue specialized education.

Liberal Arts Education That Is Too General

1. Demonstrate knowledge of or desire for work in field.
2. Sell work experience and emphasize transferable skills, such as communicating, interviewing, scheduling.
3. Sell selected courses applicable to job objective.

Too Many Unrelated Jobs

1. Sell capability in a functional resume.
2. Deemphasize different jobs and dates of employment.
3. Use a "Summary of Qualifications" section to group similar experiences.

Limited Full-Time Work Experience in the Field

1. Sell your part-time, volunteer, military, and other experiences.
2. Sell your educational achievements even harder.
3. Use a functional resume format to emphasize skills.

Work Experience in Various Fields

1. Slant the work experience you have to the field you are seeking.
2. Sell your educational achievements even harder.
3. Use a functional resume format to emphasize skills.

Gap in Work Experience Record

1. Use number of years rather than dates for length of experience, and include near the end of the paragraph.
2. Use functional resume format.
3. Don't discuss time gap until you have been offered the interview.

If You Think Age May Be a Factor

1. Do not mention age in resume or cover letter.
2. Use functional resume to sell skills.
3. Emphasize recent education and/or work experience.

STUDYING THE SAMPLES IN CHAPTERS 5, 6, 7, 8

You have now taken a personal inventory of your skills and accomplishments and have determined which skills you wish to market in your job-seeking campaign. You also have determined whether you will need to use some of the special techniques discussed. But before starting on a rough draft of your resume, refer to Chapters 5, 6, 7, and 8. The sample resumes will give you many good ideas. You may not find a resume that has the same objective as yours; what you are looking for is an example that will most closely fit your needs.

If you are entering the market place for the first time or are starting over in a completely new field, you will want to study the samples in Chapter 5. If you are a person who is trying to move up the career ladder, refer to the samples in Chapter 6. In it you will find sample resumes used by persons seeking positions with greater responsibility. These include positions with management or supervisory responsibility or positions requiring a higher level of expertise. If you are a mid-career changer, Chapter 7 is for you. It contains samples of resumes for people in transition. The selection is quite varied; therefore, you should have no trouble finding a sample that most resembles your situation. Last, Chapter 8 contains resumes for special purposes. If you are a displaced worker, a foreign-born person, a veteran, a person with a disability, a person returning to work, or an older worker, you will find an example of each type that you can model your own resume after. Take the time to study a number of resumes in each chapter to get a general idea of how to proceed with your first rough draft. Put a paper clip or corner mark on those you might want to recheck later.

PUTTING IT ALL TOGETHER

The process of putting your own material together is the focus of all the effort you have put into each of the areas covered in Chapters 1, 2, and 3. As you now begin to draft your own resume, refer back to the samples you examined and marked to restudy after completing Chapter 3. These resumes have gotten jobs for others. Use their success to your benefit! Some particular item, phrasing, or feature included in a sample resume (even one not specifically focused toward your individual circumstances) may in fact hold the key that allows you to put it all together.

Completing your own resume involves several distinct stages, each of which deserves careful attention. The discussion on format and length forms the basis for structuring your rough draft. The rough draft is the most important and the most time-consuming single stage of the entire resume-writing process, so it deserves special attention. Editing the rough draft and developing a final copy for reproduction complete the process. The final product is your strongest sales tool for use throughout the job-seeking campaign.

FORMAT

After you have decided on a style of resume that best meets your career objective, you will want to consider format. Study the accompanying examples. Which one looks most pleasing to you? Which one will best accommodate the information you have compiled? Arrangement of the information on the page should be attractive and well balanced. Again, there is no one format to be used by all.

Example 1 is attractively balanced on the page. It works particularly well for individuals who need to highlight portions of their work experience for greater impact. The key words on the left lead the reader into the paragraph further describing the objective, experience, education, personal accomplishments, and so on. Because we read from left to right, the information on the left catches our eye first.

Example 2 is also attractively balanced on the page, but it contains more information. This might best be used by those with extensive work experience pertinent to the job objective. The title of the position is placed on the left, and the name of the employer is placed on the right. It is important to accent *what* you did rather than where you did it; therefore, the reader should be led from left to right in stating what and *where*. The accompanying paragraph should further state *how*.

SAMPLE FORMATS

Example 1

Example 2

Example 3

Example 4

Example 3 might best be used for a functional resume. It presents the Summary of Qualifications paragraph at the top. Sub-heads are aligned in the left margin, with the accompanying paragraph under it. The paragraphs can be either blocked or indented.

Example 4 has major heads centered on the page with paragraphs blocked at the left margin. This style is a favorite among first-time workers and others with limited work experience. It serves to spread out the information over the page. It also appears well-balanced and is pleasing to the eye.

This book contains many examples using various formats. In addition, templates for basic resume styles are available in some word processing programs. Choose one that appeals to you and seems appropriate for your resume. A basic point is to keep the side, top, and bottom margins of a standard 8 1/2" x 11" sheet of paper at no less than 1". This white space serves as a border or "picture frame."

LENGTH

How long should the resume be? Many people say, "The information should all fit on one page!" Others say, "No more than two pages long!" There really is no consensus on what the ideal length should be. Probably the best principle to follow in determining proper length would be "the most persuasive message in as little space as possible." A message may require at least two pages, and to shorten it to one page would be to short-change the applicant and perhaps mislead readers. Rarely do circumstances warrant going into a third page. If a third page is used, it probably will be a continuation of a section that is important to the job objective. Employers tend to be turned off by a long, drawn-out resume. More skill is needed to summarize one's abilities and credentials and present them in a clear, concise manner than to go on for pages with lists. Therefore, keep your resume as short as possible.

ROUGH DRAFT

Now is the time for you to begin putting it all together. The rough draft is your first step toward the final resume. This rough draft should allow you to put your ideas into print. If the format you choose first doesn't work well, try alternative formats and arrangements until you are satisfied with the product. Working on a personal computer will allow you to keep paragraphs on disk, which can be cut and pasted in a variety of combinations to serve several purposes. You also will be able to see how the parts fit together and how they appear on the page.

Each of the following three chapters contains annotation before and after resumes. Study those examples. You will want to do the same editing with your resume. Critique your resume using the critique form to jot down ways to improve your resume. If you do not wish to critique it yourself, take it to someone who is experienced in the area of resume writing. Many times you are too close to your work to recognize where you can improve it.

Resume Critique Form

	Excellent	Good	Average	Poor
1. **Appearance.** Does it *invite* someone to read it?				
2. **Format.** Are the key points attractively placed on the page?				
3. **Actuals.** Does it state what you have actually done?				
4. **Trends.** Does it imply you are keeping up with trends (e.g. recent education, computer knowledge)?				
5. **Plan.** Does it show initiative?				
6. **Grasp.** Does it indicate you have a grasp of your field?				
7. **Positive Image.** Does it accentuate the positive and eliminate the negative?				
8. **Positive Contribution.** Does it show how you contributed during previous employment?				
9. **Positive Appeal.** Do you "toot your own horn?"				
10. **Competition.** Will it make you stand out among others?				

FINAL COPY AND REPRODUCTION

The resume in final form should be on 8 1/2" x 11" bond paper. Employers tend to prefer white or off-white shades. Avoid using darker shades of paper, as they are harder to read.

The clean, crisp appearance produced by laser printers has become the standard for resumes. If your resume does not have that look, it will stand out negatively. After all the time and effort you spent preparing your resume, you will want your professionalism to show in the end product.

Even if you do not own a personal computer, this important tool may be available to you through a local college, a nearby quick-print shop, a friend, or some other source. Producing your resume on a personal computer offers the distinct advantage of being able to rewrite and reformat as necessary. You will be able to choose from a variety of typefaces, use boldface and italics, and control the spacing of the material.

Another advantage is that you can store one or more copies of your resume on disk and thus have it available for updating and revising at a moment's notice. You may find that you need several versions of your resume, depending on job requirements, each of which can be produced with minimal changes to your stored version.

Several quick-print service centers offer desktop publishing services at reasonable prices. In addition, some quick-print centers rent word processing equipment by the hour, or you can bring your own disk to a copy center for printing. It is a good idea to keep your resume on a disk so it can be quickly updated in response to job opportunities. Check your local Yellow Pages for the name of a copy center near you. Even though you may wish to run off a limited number of copies on a copy machine available to you, you also should check with a copying service or quick-print shop. These services offer a wide paper selection with matching envelopes at reasonable prices, and they produce top quality multiple copies without any blemishes to detract from the content of your resume.

5 RESUMES FOR ENTRY-LEVEL JOB SEEKERS

ENTRY-LEVEL POSITIONS

"Entry-level," as used in this manual, refers to the beginning point of a position. The person applying for an entry-level position is often a first-time worker, a high school graduate, or a college graduate with an associate's, bachelor's, or master's degree. "Entry-level position" can refer to first-level management, which might be either supervisory or trainee, or it can refer to positions in sales, data processing, and various technical fields in which on-the-job training is requisite. The applicant for such a position might be trying to break into a field with a degree equivalent in experience and nonformal or specialized training. Whether your qualifications come from recent education or from previous work experience, the techniques for writing the resume are similar.

Another way to break into a field and bridge the gap between education and work is through an internship program. A resume designed for a person desiring an internship position is included on page 56 in this chapter.

Job seekers often fail to realize that each company or institution has its own policies and procedures and that an employee often has to start at a lower level of employment and work up. For example, a person seeking a position in management may have to begin as a trainee to become familiar with the company. If all goes well, promotions take place as the individual learns the various phases of the business or institution. Accenting your transferable skills and indicating a willingness to learn new skills can enhance your chances of being promoted.

SAMPLE RESUMES

The first two sample resumes in this chapter are Before and After versions. The circled numerals in the Before version refer to the following list, which points out problem areas in the resume. The After version shows the same resume after improvements have been made. The remaining pages of the chapter contain sample resumes for entry-level positions.

Problem Areas in Stuart G. Foster's Resume

1. No objective is listed in the Before version. Most employers do not want to fit the person to the job; the applicant should know what position he or she is applying for. (See employer comments in Chapter 12.)

2. No location is given for any of the employment entries in the Before version. Inclusion of this data is important, as the employer will want to make reference checks later.

3. Several transferable skills in this military position should be highlighted. These are taken out and placed in a "Qualifications" section in the After version of this resume. The section on military experience was not omitted or abbreviated, because it shows a great deal of responsibility for a person of this age. (Incidentally, Stuart *did* get the position, and the employer *was* impressed with his military background.)

4. This special military training could be omitted, as it does not apply to the civilian position Stuart is applying for.

5. The reference to high school should be omitted, as it is no longer applicable.

**Sample Resume:
Before Version**

STUART G. FOSTER
4030 Camino del Rio South
San Diego, CA 92101
(619) 230-1561

EMPLOYMENT

10/95 to
Present

Commercial Fence
Position: Foreman

Acquire contracts; estimate jobs; order parts and supplies.
Supervise two persons.

EMPLOYMENT ②

9/93
to
9/95

Attached to Air Anti–Submarine Squadron 38 deployed 2/95 to
8/95 on board USS RANGER (CV–61). Responsibilities included
③ planning, editing, keystroking all instructions, awards, correspondence, and related training materials. Collection and distribution
of all official and personal mail. Leading Airman of the First
Lieutenant Division. Duties included maintaining material condition of Squadron and Hangar spaces. Supervised five members of
staff. Secret Clearance.

EMPLOYMENT ②

1/92
to
2/93

El Torito Restaurant
Position: Waiter

Responsible for quick and friendly service to customers. Assigned
various tasks normally involved in the restaurant business.

EDUCATION

Grossmont College, El Cajon, CA	1996
Navy Alcohol, Drug and Safety Course	June 1994
Plane Captain School	May 1994
Shipboard Aircraft Firefighting School	April 1994
Airman Apprenticeship Training	December 1993
Diploma, Lakewood High School,	
Lakewood, CA	June 1994

④

⑤

HONORS

Sailor of the Month	May 1994
Letter of Appreciation	August 1995

REFERENCES   Available Upon Request

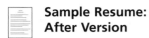

Sample Resume:
After Version

STUART G. FOSTER
4030 Camino del Rio South
San Diego, California 92101
(619) 230-1561

OBJECTIVE
Accounting Clerk

QUALIFICATIONS

ORGANIZATION AND MANAGEMENT — Planned, edited, keystroked, and distributed daily periodical. Supervised members of staff.

WORD PROCESSING — Processed all instructions, awards and related instructions using word processing equipment.

CLERICAL/ ACCOUNTING — Currently studying Accounting and Microsoft Excel.

EDUCATION

Grossmont College, El Cajon, CA. Working toward A.A. transfer degree in Business Administration (Accounting). Presently enrolled in 101-A Accounting and Microsoft Excel.

EMPLOYMENT HISTORY

<u>Foreman</u>
Commercial Fence, Cerritos, CA

Job estimating and fence installation, order parts and supplies, supervise labor apprentice. (October 1995 to present)

<u>Nondesignated Airman</u>
United States Navy, San Diego, CA

Attached to Air Anti-Submarine Squadron 38 deployed 2/95 to 8/95 on board USS Ranger (CV-61). Responsibilities included planning, editing, typing, and distribution of Squadron Daily Periodical (Plan of the Day). Maintained Officers' Service Records. Word processed all instructions, awards, correspondence, and official and personal mail. Leading Airman of the First Lieutenant Division; duties included maintaining material condition of Squadron and Hangar spaces. Supervised five members of staff. Secret Clearance. (September 1993 to September 1995)

<u>Waiter</u>
El Torito Restaurant, Lakewood, CA

Responsible for quick and friendly service to customers. Assigned various tasks normally involved in the restaurant business. (January 1992 to February 1993)

HONORS

Sailor of the Month - May 1994   Letter of Appreciation - August 1995

Sample Resume:
Entry-Level

MARY LOU BETTS

Present Address	*Permanent Address*
821 Magnolia Lane #41	114 Summit Drive
Austin, Texas 78752	Birmingham, Alabama 35235
(512) 371-6801	(205) 325-8101

OBJECTIVE
To acquire an entry-level position in marketing leading to a position in management based on my performance.

EDUCATION
University of Texas at Austin. 1995 to present
Major: Marketing. Expected graduation: May 1997.
50% of tuition earned while working 20–30 hours weekly.
Jefferson State Junior College, Birmingham, Alabama
Major: Communications—1993 to 1995.

SKILLS
Marketing coordination, bookkeeping, retail sales, computer operation, customer and employee relations.

EXPERIENCE
Tex's Steak House—Austin, Texas—Summer 1996
BOOKKEEPER. Responsible for general ledger accounting for a dinner house averaging $50,000 weekly income, AR/AP, bank and credit card deposits.

Monica's Fashions—Austin, Texas—Summer 1996
SALES CLERK. Retail sales for an exclusive boutique; developed display utilizing a one-to-one person shopping method.

Jeffery P. Stoddard, CPA—Austin, Texas—Summer 1995
MARKETING CLERK. In charge of all marketing activities, including preparing and coordinating seminars, maintaining and updating client mailing lists for dissemination of the monthly newsletter, specifying and contacting new target markets through brochures and cold calls. Increased client file by 20%.

Creative Concepts, Inc.—Birmingham, Alabama—1/94–5/95
BOOKKEEPER. Responsibilities included AP/AR, auditing all in-house transactions, cash management, customer and employee problems, and operating the central computer system.

ACHIEVEMENTS
University: American Marketing Association, Finance Association, Delta Gamma Sorority, U.T. Fashion Group member and model, Texas Cowgirls member, Honor Roll student.

REFERENCES
Available upon request.

Sample Resume:
Entry-Level

KENYA SWAIN

520 Taft Avenue, Orange, California 92665
714/974-9001

OBJECTIVE	ANIMAL HEALTH TECHNICIAN. Wish to begin career in animal health field by preparing pharmaceuticals, conducting lab tests on blood/urine specimens, and performing general laboratory skills.
EXPERIENCE	Worked for two summers at Villa Park Animal Hospital, Villa Park, transferring and returning animals from housing area to the working surface; correctly restraining the animal so there was minimum movement while administering injection; and assisting vet during surgical procedures done under general anesthetic. (1995–1996)
SPECIAL SKILLS	General laboratory skills. Small animal care and maintenance. Entry-level proficiency in sample preparation, use of volumetric glassware, biochemical and media preparation, biohazards and use of electronic instruments.
EDUCATION	A.A. Degree (Biological Technician), Fullerton College, California, June, 1994.
	Major courses included: General Biology, Introduction to Chemistry, Technical Mathematics, Survey of Electronics, Biological Techniques and Applications, Scientific Instrumentation, Scientific Communications.
SPECIAL TRAINING	Completed a course in "Veterinary Hospital Practice," which included observation in a veterinary hospital and lecture/discussions designed to introduce students to various facets of hospital procedures. The topics included animal care and handling, laboratory chemical analysis, parasitology, pharmacy and nutrition, preparation and administration of drugs, X-ray procedures, medical nursing, and emergency procedures.
OTHER FACTS	Enjoy all sports . . . an animal lover . . . like to be assigned challenging jobs involving important results and requiring imaginative solutions.

Sample Resume:
Entry-Level

BETTINA GALLO
2902 Mockingbird Lane
Dallas, Texas 75205
(214) 669-2201

OBJECTIVE	Management Trainee position in an Auto Parts Store where technical skills, training abilities, and leadership capabilities can be demonstrated.

EXPERIENCE

United States Affiliated   Fort Worth, Texas

Sole operator of repair facility serving the painting industry. Started with an empty building and planned and designed service center for efficient operation. Performed extensive public relations. Competition forced me to terminate the business. Became a full-time student. (1996–1997).

Bell Paint Company   Fort Worth, Texas

Organized and designed the service department. Designed easy access parts inventory to aid salespeople. Taught customers the operation of spray equipment and initiated equipment rental program. Purchased equipment and products. (1994–1996).

Grenoble Lincoln-Mercury   Dallas, Texas

Performed sales and service to cars at exhaust repair department. Inspected new cars before they were sold. Followed specific instructions as set forth by manager. (1992–1994).

EDUCATION

Currently working toward an A.A. Degree in Business Management at Richland College. Long-range plans are to transfer to the University of Texas at Austin for a B.S. Degree in Business Administration.

SPECIAL ACCOMPLISHMENTS

Solved Bell Paint Company's adjustment problem with its Model ST8000 airless pump, which had plagued the company for three years. This cut the average repair time from 2 1/2 hours to 45 minutes. Very few repairpersons mastered the repairs on these diaphragm pumps.

OTHER FACTS

I can handle impromptu situations dealing with people. I possess the ability to visualize and troubleshoot problems. I am willing to relocate.

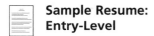 **Sample Resume:
Entry-Level**

ERIC W. BRIDGEMAN

5005 Colgate Avenue   (303) 527-3534
Boulder, Colorado 80303

OBJECTIVE

Computer Aided Design Position

QUALIFICATIONS

CAD Operation—Received training on "virtual reality" software. Invested 300 hours in lab study.

PCB Drafting and Design—Designed analog and digital boards. Became familiar with component catalogs and industry's standards. Developed crib sheets, transmittals, assembly drawings, and board details.

Electronic Packaging Design—Became familiar with the procedures of designing rack-and-panels, P.C.B. enclosures, black boxes, and cable assemblies.

Electronic Drafting—Developed a thorough understanding of the technique and requirements of schematics, block, wiring, and logic diagrams.

Industrial Drafting—Instructed in the proper use of dimensions, tolerances, and views on production details and assembly drawing.

Technical Illustration—Developed the art of isometric drawings (usually in ink).

WORK EXPERIENCE

Design Draftsperson   James General Engineering
                                                                 Denver, Colorado

Designed cable T.V. street, apartment, and condo lines. Designed electronics and mapping lines. (1997)

N/C Computer Operator   Shelton Circuits
                                                                 Boulder, Colorado

Received training in N/C drilling machines. Ran and maintained Excellon Mark 5 Driller. (1996)

Machinist Department Head   Motor Mart
                                                                 Boulder, Colorado

Rebuilt engine heads from engine tear-down to final assembly. (1995)

EDUCATION

Arapahoe Community College, Littleton, Colorado. A.A. Degree, Electronics Technical, June 1997. Grade Point Average—3.7.

REFERENCES

Available upon request.

Sample Resume:
Entry-Level

CARLOS R. RAMIREZ **(714) 547-9400**	**1908 Baker, Apt. 9** **Santa Ana, California 92703**

OBJECTIVE:	To help a retail company provide high customer satisfaction while managing merchandise efficiently in an entry-level management position.
SKILLS:	Resolved customer problems in retail merchandising. Organized product floor for customer convenience. Experienced in dealing with wholesalers. Organized and maintained inventories. College courses in management, personnel, finance, statistics, and marketing.
EDUCATION:	California State University, Fullerton, California B.S., Business Administration, May 1996, Management Emphasis
HONORS:	Academic Scholarship; Delta Mu Delta (Business Honorary)
ACTIVITIES AND MEMBERSHIPS:	Youth Leader of a 60-member church youth group; Student Senator; Photography Club

RELEVANT EXPERIENCE

FEB. 1996–PRESENT	WESTERN GRAPHICS ASSOCIATES, Fullerton, California Graphic Arts - Delivery Person. Master all aspects of pre-press operations. Effectively deal with and resolve conflicts. Oversee various camera procedures including working with numerous types of film and preparing press plates.
FEB. 1995–FEB. 1996	CONTINENTAL GRAPHICS, Santa Ana, California Graphic Arts - Delivery Person. Demonstrated ability to serve and communicate with customers in a diverse office-supply operation. Organized and maintained product floor and inventory.
JUN. 1993–MAY 1995	AMC THEATERS, Fullerton, California Projectionist. Promoted four times within a two-year period. Operated six projectors simultaneously with a high degree of efficiency; stripped, broke down, and kept films clean.
ADDITIONAL INFORMATION:	Paid 100% of college expenses Worked to support wife and child while attending college full-time. Computer training includes BASIC, COBOL, Assembler, and "C."
REFERENCES:	Available upon request.

Sample Resume:
Entry-Level

GREGORY PETERSON
421 East Main Street
Fargo, North Dakota 58102
(701) 624-7310

OBJECTIVE: *Machinist*

EDUCATION: A.A. Degree, Machine Shop, North Dakota School of Science, Wahpeton, North Dakota. June, 1993. Major Courses: four semesters' Machine shop, two semesters' Technical Math, two semesters' Welding, Introduction to Numerical Control, Fundamentals of Metallurgy, Fundamentals of Drafting, and Manufacturing Processes.

SPECIAL
SKILLS: *Lathes.* Experience in the setup and operation of the following machines: Clausing Colchester 13" w/digital readout, Cincinnati Hydrashift 12", Sidney 16", Regal 18", DoAll 13", Leblond 12", Zubal, Reed-Prentice, Cincinnati Traytop 12 1/2 x 36.

Mills. Experience on the large Cincinnati Horizontal with auto-feed, Milwaukee Model H with auto-feed, Cincinnati Vertical with auto-feed, and Millrite vertical with auto-feed and digital readout.

Drill Presses. Operated standard drill presses and a Morris Mor-Speed radial arm drill press. Related drill press setups included use of V-blocks, vises, taping, counterboring, countersinking, and use of centerfinder to locate holes.

Grinding. Operated Gallmeyer & Livingston surface grinder, Thompson surface grinder, Sanford Model MG dry surface grinder, and Brown & Sharp cylindrical grinder.

WORK
EXPERIENCE: *Department Manager*   Solutions Unlimited
Shipping, Receiving and Finishing   Fargo, ND
Supervised four people in packaging, shipping, and assembly of printed material and displays. Operated Thompson 28 x 41 die cutter, Seybold 65" paper cutter, laminator, slitter, table saw, and forklift. In charge of customer orders and inventory. (1993–1996)

Maintenance Man   Rodger's Trucking Company
                        Fargo, ND
Parked and operated refrigeration systems of company trucks. Provided preventative maintenance to all company vehicles and forklifts. Part-time while attending college. (1992)

OTHER FACTS: Willing to relocate. Machinery interest carries over to complete maintenance of motorcycle and 4-wheel drive vehicles. Have some machinist tools.

Sample Resume:
Entry-level

EMILY D. JENSEN
1430 Imperial Drive
Joliet, Illinois 60435
(312) 691-4580

OBJECTIVE

Position as a Computer Software Designer and Programmer in a growing company.

EXPERIENCE

Programmer   Applied Microsystems, Inc.
                                                                    Champaign, Illinois

Wrote new programs for medical billing and maintained existing programs using HP 3000, COBOL II with MPE. Duties include logic flowcharts, verifying program logic by preparing test data for trial runs; tested and debugged programs; prepared instruction sheet to guide computer operations during production runs; prepared documentation procedures. (January 1996–February 1997)

Programmer Trainee   American Savings and Loan
                                                                    Association
                                                                    Joliet, Illinois

Upgraded existing mortgage programs. Revised program table and wrote documentation procedures and a new program using TOTAL 7 database. Verified program logic by preparing test data for trial runs. Tested and debugged programs. (Internship 1995)

Applications Programming Trainee   TransAmerica Information Systems
                                                                    Joliet, Illinois

Assisted in development and installation of the software package DATAMANAGER, entered data and produced reports. (Internship 1993)

EDUCATION

A.S degree in Information Systems and Computer Programming from Parkland College, Champaign-Urbana, Illinois (1994–1996).

Introduction to Networking and   Accounting (101A, 101B)
   Telecommunications   Programming in C
Cobol Programming (214A, 214B)   Pascal Programming
Microsoft Excel for Windows   dBase on the PC (Beginning and
Finite Business Math   Advanced)
BASIC Programming   Document Imaging and Management

REFERENCES

Available upon request

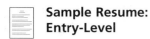

Sample Resume:
Entry-Level

Jim 'Ryder' Anderson
217 W. Fairchild Avenue
Santa Ana, California 92706
(714) 557-4974

OBJECTIVE

To obtain a position in radio as a News/Sports Announcer.

EXPERIENCE

On-Air Personality, News/Sports Director   KAJZ-FM
Los Angeles, CA

Responsible for producing sports information and radio shows; gather needed materials including news/sports data, music lists, features and content, and actual play-by-play and color analysis of games. (1995 to present)

Station Manager, Music/Program Director,   KPFK-FM
Air Talent   Los Angeles, CA

Duties involve overseeing all station functions including hiring and training personnel, scheduling of talent and specialty shows, and preparing reports and budget agendas for board review. (1993 to present)

Production Assistant   KNAC-FM
Los Angeles, CA

Involved in all aspects of commercial production including recording and editing of announcers' materials, supplying appropriate music beds and dubbing onto proper broadcast components. (August 1994 to June 1995)

Disc Jockey, Promotions Director   Harvey's Bar & Grill
Omaha, NE

Responsible for coordinating talent, organizing music and promotional schedules, and preparing timely shows for an average audience of 100. (1992 to 1994)

SPECIAL KNOWLEDGE

- Copywriting
- 4-24 Track Production
- Voice-Overs
- AP News Desk 2.0
- News/Sportscasting
- DBX 163 Processor
- Management
- Eventide Harmonizer

EDUCATION

Metropolitan Technical Community College, Omaha, NE. Completed courses for Radio Certificate, June 1992.
A.A. Degree in communications, December 1991, 3.3 GPA.

HONORS

Received Associated Students' *Certificate of Award* for managing student radio station, KMTC 93.5 FM.
Nominated *Man of Distinction* for communications, student government, and service to college.

Sample Resume:
Entry-Level

RANJAN SARAF

<u>Present Address</u>

8927 Penn Street, Apt. 22
Houston, Texas 77002
(713) 527-9710

<u>Permanent Address</u>

2630 Fairford Drive
Lafayette, Louisiana 70508
(318) 417-1980

OBJECTIVE
Manufacturing Engineer—Machine Design in the energy industry.

EDUCATION
Candidate for B.S. degree in Mechanical Engineering Technology, University of Houston Central Campus, May 1997. Major emphasis in mechanical design. G.P.A.: 3.5 in major; 3.1 overall. Base - 4.0.

Coursework has included: strength of materials, applied dynamics, kinematics of mechanisms, materials and processes, design of mechanisms, and tool design

San Jacinto Junior College, Pasadena, Texas. Completed thirty hours with a G.P.A. of 3.5/4.0. 1994–95.

Seventy-five percent of expenses earned from scholarships and employment

SCHOLARSHIPS AND HONORS
Treasurer, Golden Key National Honor Society
Tau Alpha Pi National Honor Society Academic scholarship from San Jacinto Junior College

EXPERIENCE
Draftsperson, Gulf Oil Company, Houston, Texas
Responsibilities included drafting of down hole tools and equipment. Initially hired as a tracer, detailer and later promoted. September 1995–January 1996

Machine Operator, Reed Tool Company, Houston, Texas. 1994–95

Shipping clerk, lifeguard, grocery cashier, and stocker, part-time and summer employment. 1992–94

ACTIVITIES
Vice President, Society of Manufacturing Engineers
Intramural athletics

REFERENCES
Available upon request

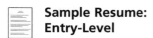

Sample Resume:
Entry-Level

SABRINA OROS

1234 West First Street
Fullerton, California 92631
(714) 522-3433

OBJECTIVE Attorney

BAR California State Bar, November, 1996
MEMBERSHIP

WORK
EXPERIENCE

1995–96 **Law Clerk**—Orange County Public Defender's Office.
Conducted minor crime investigations upon attorney's
request; served subpoenas; interviewed witnesses and
prepared investigation reports.

1994–95 **Law Clerk**—Berg & Keller, Santa Ana, California.
Prepared interrogatories and trial briefs; drafted pleadings
and performed field investigations.

1994 **Law Clerk**—Hanson, Levy & Price, Tustin, California.
Researched legal issues; prepared pleadings and motions
and interviewed witnesses.

1991–93 **Shift Production Supervisor**—Lindon, Inc., Irvine, California.
Coordinated shift operations; increased production 100
percent over a period of six months and heightened the
level of personal commitment of the individual employee.

EDUCATION Western State University College of Law, Fullerton, California.
Juris Doctor degree, May 1996.
Class Standing: Top 15 percent.
• Dean's Honor Roll
• American Jurisprudence Award—Torts
• Moot Court, National Competition
• Member, Handicapped Students' Association

California State University, Fullerton, California.
Bachelor of Science in Political Science, 1986.
• Who's Who Among Students in American Colleges and
Universities

REFERENCES Available Upon Request

Sample Resume:
Entry-Level

ERIC CHANG
2001 La Veta Avenue, #301
Orange, California 92667

OBJECTIVE
Naturalist Internship, Santiago Canyon Nature Center

QUALIFICATIONS

Landscape/Nursery Management
- Administered various cultural techniques of soil preparation, planting, pruning, watering, and fertilization to a diversity of plant types.
- Educated in cultural, soil, and climatical needs of a multitude of plants.
- Trained in a variety of propagation techniques and greenhouse and nursery management skills.
- Knowledgeable in landscape design and construction practices.
- Knowledgeable in the common and Latin names and growth requirements of trees, shrubs, ground covers, and herbaceous plants.

Work Habits
- Highly persistent, self-motivated, and self-directed toward attaining the completion of tasks and projects.
- Skilled in working as a team member in production setting.

Personal Interests
- Ecology/Wildlife gardens, water gardens, garden design, backpacking, and fishing.

EDUCATION

Orange Coast College, Costa Mesa, California. 1992–present
Working toward transfer degree in Park Administration. Major coursework completed includes Principles of Horticulture, Plant Identification, Trees and Shrubs, Applied Botany, Plant Propagation, Landscape Design, Advanced Landscape Design, Dry Climate Landscaping, Zoology, and Mountain Top Ecology I and II.

Goals and Highlights of Qualifications
- Park Administration with emphasis in natural resources.
- 4.0 GPA in major: President's Honor List (1992–1994).

Central Orange County Regional Occupational Program
- Certificates: Landscape/Nursery and Floral Design (1992).

EMPLOYMENT HISTORY

Los Angeles County Arboretum   Arcadia, CA
Horticulture Internship
Practiced pruning trees and shrubs; prepared soil and planted landscape areas; propagated, shifted, and repotted nursery plants; assisted with construction projects (1994).

Flowerdale Nurseries, Inc.   Santa Ana, California
Machine operator on the production line. A team member and trained as a leader.

6 RESUMES FOR PEOPLE SEEKING ADVANCEMENT

**MAKE YOUR PAST
ACHIEVEMENTS
WORK FOR YOU**

What do you do when you feel you have outgrown your present job? Many people become restless and look for new responsibility and challenge. Sometimes this challenge can be met within the same organization in which you currently work. Therefore, it is advisable that you first discuss career opportunities with your immediate supervisor or personnel manager. Often people are passed up for promotion simply because they failed to call attention to their past achievements.

People interested in making career advancements might be entry-level workers desiring positions with management or supervisory responsibility or positions requiring higher levels of expertise, such as a word processing clerk moving up to a secretarial position. Other people interested in moving up might be manager trainees whose objective is middle-level management. Middle-level managers might wish to be heads of departments such as accounting, sales, purchasing, marketing, data processing, personnel, and research and development. Higher-level individuals might aspire to become executives on an administrative level. This includes high-level posts in business and industry, local, state, and federal agencies, and nonprofit organizations of many kinds.

Sample resumes in this chapter include a part-time electronics instructor seeking a full-time position; a secretary aspiring to a position as a wage and salary analyst; a systems engineer hoping for a position as a systems analyst; a dietitian seeking a position as a director of dietetic services; a sales and marketing assistant looking for a hotel management position; and an operations manager wanting a position as plant manager. All of these examples highlight work experience in such a way as to give proof that the individual is qualified for a position with more responsibility.

The sample resume for a biochemistry position with management responsibility (Jason Woo) utilizes the functional style to highlight qualifications before discussing the employment history. This serves to place the applicant's previous management responsibilities at the beginning of the resume while the reader is forming an opinion of the applicant's qualifications. The example depicts how an individual with a degree in biological sciences and education can market himself/herself in industry. This sample resume also shows how you can redirect your career goals if you are unable to obtain a teaching position or have difficulty getting admitted to professional school (e.g., medicine, dentistry, veterinary medicine).

Regardless of the level of position the person is aiming for, some statistics about the labor market must be considered. As discussed in Chapter 2, the labor market can be divided into two sections: the published and the unpublished. The published section consists of jobs advertised in the newspapers, jobs listed with college placement centers, and jobs that can be obtained through employment agencies or recruiters. The unpublished section represents approximately 75–80 percent of the labor market. In the unpublished area, about half of the jobs are potential jobs, not current jobs. These jobs have to be created. All job seekers—especially people who wish to move up—should be aware of these statistics.

In summary, when writing a resume designed for upward mobility, you must communicate your effectiveness on previous jobs and relate how these achievements make you qualified to handle the higher position. It is also to your distinct advantage to inform your potential employer of new appropriate qualifications acquired since your last resume was completed.

SAMPLE RESUMES

The first two sample resumes are Before and After versions, with areas of change noted on the Before version. The circled numerals in the Before version refer to the following list, which points out problem areas in the resume. The After version shows the same resume after improvements have been made. The remaining pages in the chapter contain sample resumes for people seeking career advancement.

Problem Areas in the Scott T. Gusman Resume

1. The words "confidential resume" indicate to the recipient that Scott is currently employed and does not want anyone to contact his present employer. This can probably go unsaid since this issue usually is dealt with during the interview; after all, searching for a job while employed is a common practice.

2. The Summary of Qualifications is lengthy and could be considered overkill. Qualifications summaries should constitute a broad summing up of various experiences that have taken place over five or more years. A personal statement, if used, should be simple and to the point. Most employers prefer seeing this type of information in a cover letter (see employers' comments in Chapter 12).

3. The reader has to wade through the paragraph to determine what Scott accomplished on the job. A device such as bullets leads the reader through the skills and accomplishments one at a time and also makes the resume easier to scan.

4. Although this position is not directly related to Scott's objective, it does imply that he has had a great deal of public contact, which is an asset for a sales representative.

5. Personal information of this nature should not be included on a resume.

6. The subject of compensation is best left for negotiation during the interview and need not be mentioned on the resume.

Sample Resume:
Before Version

SCOTT T. GUSMAN
3891 Harvard Avenue
Redondo Beach, CA 90277

 CONFIDENTIAL RESUME

(213) 316-9201

SUMMARY OF QUALIFICATIONS

A combination of formal education, specialized training, and practical application has resulted in excellent qualifications in **MANAGEMENT, SALES, PUBLIC RELATIONS**, and **CUSTOMER SERVICE**. Command excellent communication skills, both written and verbal. Interface well with individuals of diverse and varied backgrounds. Goal-oriented and take pride in meeting and exceeding objectives.

Excel in the supervision and management of time and personnel, with special skill in coordinating multiple projects simultaneously. Work efficiently and resourcefully in pressure situations, making critical decisions with sound judgment. Quickly establish and maintain a strong working rapport with all levels of management and co-workers as well as customers. Present a professional attitude and appearance at all times.

PROFESSIONAL EXPERIENCE

SALES MANAGER/PRODUCTION ASSISTANT

Franco, Inc.
Hawthorne, CA

Responsible for marketing and sales for manufacturer of automobile accessories. Develop new accounts as well as maintain existing customers. Oversee and train sales staff to utilize effective sales techniques to increase profitability and augment a high standard of service. In addition, troubleshoot and resolve production problems in accordance with customer specifications. Travel to off-road functions to promote products. (1995 to Present)

LAB TECHNICIAN/SUPERVISOR

Bridgford Foods Corporation
Anaheim, CA

Supervised staff of seven technicians at a food processing and distributing plant. Delegated workload and maintained schedule. Analyzed data for inclusion into quality control and production management reports to upper management. In addition, performed inventory control and ordering of supplies. Assisted in preparing payroll and associated accounting duties. Utilized knowledge of Lotus 1-2-3 for data entry and analysis. (1994 to 1995)

SALESPERSON

Cameo P.C.
El Segundo, CA

Successfully marketed IBM computers by educating and answering questions over the phone in response to nationwide advertising through specialty computer magazines. Gained a broad knowledge of software and hardware capabilities. (1984 to 1994)

Scott T. Gusman   Page 2

OFFICE COMMUNICATIONS COORDINATOR   U.C.L.A. Publications
                                                         Los Angeles, CA

Performed on-call distribution for University Publishing Department. (1994)

(4) HOST/WAITER   Reuben's Restaurant
                                                         Marina del Rey, CA

Held this part-time job while attending college.

EDUCATIONAL BACKGROUND

B.A. Degree—University of California, Los Angeles (1995)
Major: History   Minor: Psychology

PERSONAL INFORMATION

(5) Excellent Health—Born: 7/3/71—Height: 5'11"
Weight: 170 lbs

Willing to Travel/Relocate

REFERENCES: Available upon request   (6) COMPENSATION: Open to
                                                 Negotiation

Sample Resume:
After Version

SCOTT T. GUSMAN
3891 Harvard Avenue
Redondo Beach, California 90277
(213) 316-9201

OBJECTIVE: Sales Representative

PROFESSIONAL EXPERIENCE

Sales Manager/Production Assistant   Franco, Inc.
                                                                        Hawthorne, CA

- Responsible for marketing and sales for manufacturer of automobile accessories.
- Develop new accounts as well as maintain existing customers.
- Monitor and train sales staff to utilize effective sales techniques to increase profitability and augment a high standard of service.
- Troubleshoot and resolve production problems in accordance with customer specifications.
- Travel to off-road functions to promote products. (1995 to present)

Lab Technician/Supervisor   Bridgford Foods Corporation
                                                                        Anaheim, CA

- Supervised staff of seven technicians.
- Delegated workload and maintained schedule.
- Analyzed data for inclusion into quality control and production management reports to upper management.
- Performed inventory control and ordered supplies.
- Utilized knowledge of Lotus 1-2-3. (1994–1995)

Salesperson   Cameo P.C.
                                                                        El Segundo, CA

- Successfully marketed IBM computers by educating customers and answering telephone questions in response to nationwide advertising through specialty computer magazines. (1993–1994)

Office Communications Coordinator   UCLA Publications
                                                                     Los Angeles, CA

- Performed on-call distribution for University Publishing Department. (1994)

Host/Waiter   Reuben's Restaurant
                                                                    Marina del Rey, CA

- Held this part-time job while attending UCLA.

EDUCATION

B. A. Degree—University of California, Los Angeles (1995)
Major: History   Minor: Psychology

REFERENCES

Available upon Request

**Sample Resume:
Seeking Career
Advancement**

RICHARD R. GILDAR

421 Pine Canyon Drive
Eugene, Oregon 97405
(503) 918-4015
r_gildar@enet.net

OBJECTIVE:	Full-time position as an instructor in electronics.
SUMMARY OF QUALIFICATIONS:	More than 20 years of professional experience in engineering, technical training, and consulting capacities. Author of text-books on digital electronics and computer technology.

PROFESSIONAL
EXPERIENCE:

Instructor/Coordinator   1992 to Present
Lane Community College and Lane County Community College District Adult
Education, Eugene, Oregon

- Teach electronics theory, mathematics, and related laboratory for AC, DC and Digital.
- Coordinate technical aspects of E.S.L. and Special E.O.P.S. classes for students with special problems. Have also been involved with CETA and CWETA programs.
- Help students locate and obtain jobs where they successfully compete with electronic technicians with up to five years' experience.
- Maintain industrial contacts using feedback to improve curriculum.

Applications Engineer and Engineering Consultant   1992 to 1994
States Industries, Eugene, Oregon

- Directed all administrative and technical aspects of department.
- Stimulated and trained distributors and sales representatives.
- Organized distributor and representative technical and sales training seminars.
- Performed customer interface and customer problem resolution.
- Marketing activities included definition and specification of new products and new product areas.

Engineering Manager   1987 to 1992
CH2M Hill, Inc., Corvallis, Oregon

- Performed consulting tasks involving product definition, product design, testing programs, quality control, applications engineering and engineering management.

Richard R. Gildar Page 2

Engineering Specialist 1983 to 1987
Data Technology Corporation, Santa Ana, California

- Assignments included customer interface, systems definition, and quotations of A/D. D/A conversion equipment and computer systems.

- Assisted with designing, manufacturing and testing of special systems, allowing for timely delivery within specified budgets.

EDUCATION:

Working toward degree in Electrical and Computer Engineering at Oregon State University, Corvallis. Have completed 76 of the required 90 quarter hours. Graduate-level education courses include Research Design Techniques and Tests and Measurements.

PUBLICATIONS:

"Power Supplies Need Exercise, Too," published August 15, 1988, in *Electrical Design News.*

Author of textbook *Introduction to Digital Concepts* and *Laboratory Manual— Introduction to Digital Concepts and TLL Hardware,* published in 1996 by H & H Publishers, Orange, California.

SPECIAL ACCOMPLISHMENTS:

Patent disclosure: P243-E, Standard Power, Inc.

REFERENCES:

Available upon request

**Sample Resume:
Seeking Career
Advancement**

HEATHER M. PRESTON
2850 West Bellview Avenue
Littleton, Colorado 80123
(303) 332-7148

OBJECTIVE

Position as a Case Manager in a managed care facility where skills in critical thinking and communication will be an asset.

SUMMARY OF QUALIFICATIONS

Six years' diversified experience in the managed care medical field, interacting at all levels with medical professionals and patients.

EXPERIENCE AND SKILLS

Orthotics: **Patient Follow-up Specialist**   Orthotic Systems
                                                              Denver, Colorado

- Presently evaluate progress of 300–700 patients monthly.
- Identify problems; recommend and imlement solutions.
- Improved existing systems and created procedures in response to company downsizing.
- Detected and documented insurance fraud.   (1995 to present)

PPO/Utilization Review: **Administrative Assistant**   Sunrise Care
                                                              Littleton, Colorado

- Successfully reorganized procedures and implemented changes to meet aggressive cost containment policies.
- Monitored production of all printed materials; ordered supplies; maintained on- and off-site inventories.
- Coordinated production of Provider Directories; designed and prepared mass mailings to contracted providers (physicians and hospitals).   (1993 to 1995)

HMO: **Administrative Assistant**   General Med, Inc.
                                                              Denver, Colorado

- Organized, coordinated, and supervised secretarial support for Operations Division, including Clinic Management, Nursing, X-Ray, Pharmacy, and Optometry Departments.
- Routinely maintained diplomatic and effective people skills while working under deadline pressures.   (1990 to 1993)

EDUCATION

Bachelor's degree in Administration and Management (1990 to 1993)
University of Denver, Denver, Colorado

RELATED TRAINING

Connective Tissue Physiology Training Course
J. Loughlin, M.D., Loughlin Medical, Baltimore, Maryland

References available upon request.

**Sample Resume:
Seeking Career
Advancement**

D. L. (Donna) Davenport
456 Tammy Lane
Panama City, Florida, 32404
(305) 928-4201   davenport@aol.com

OBJECTIVE

To obtain a position managing complex system integration and application development projects in a commercial environment.

SKILLS

- Systems Integration Project Management
- Software Development First Line Management
- Software Engineering/Software Process

EXPERIENCE

Senior Systems Engineer   AeroTech Corporation
                                                         Fort Walton Beach, FL

Led multi-disciplinary team of fifteen members from all areas of system development in the specification, software development, formal system test, and development of customer training materials for the Simulation applications. Acted as liaison and negotiated technical agreements with the customer for the Simulation area.

- Took over the specification production effort when it was three months behind schedule and delivered the product on time. The spec production schedule was ten months total.
- Representative on the Database Review Board setting project standards for the distributed database design and documentation.
- AeroTech was awarded a $3 million Completion Bonus in 1996 for beating the forty-one month accelerated schedule by three months.

(1994–1996, Safe Haven Project; SEI rating = 4+)

Systems Engineer   AeroTech Systems International
                                                         Manchester, England

Led the Tracking Applications Team during the site sell-off phase of the project. Responsible for the update and testing of software in the areas of Radar Data Processing, Active Tracking, Passive Tracking, and Automatic Track Initiation.

- Analyzed, provided cost estimates, and led the implemention of an extensive redesign of the Active Tracking and Radar Data Processing applications necessary for sell-off.
- Negotiated the design, schedule, and test methods with the customer, led the multi-disciplinary team of five that implemented and tested the changes, and documented the results to achieve customer acceptance of the changes.
- Awarded a Management Incentive Completion Bonus for delivering the system thirteen weeks ahead of schedule.

(1991–1994, UKSafe Project; SEI rating = 3)

Systems Engineer   AeroTech Corporation
                                                         Fort Walton Beach, FL

Led the Special Applications Team of ten software engineers during the design, code, test, and integration phases of a command and control information system for Australia. The special applications included Sortie Status, Mission Planning, Rescue, and Weather.

- Integration coordinator (IC) for all applications teams during the integration phase of the project. As IC, prioritized project-wide integration resources, coordinated PERT charts, and assisted all areas with integration problems.

(1990–1991, Outback Project; SEI rating = 3)

Systems Engineer   AeroTech Systems International
                                                        Kyoto, Japan

Site specialist responsible for the testing, debugging, update, and results presentation of the Surveillance area software during on-site testing and sell-off of a large realtime system for Japan. The Surveillance applications included Radar Data Processing, Radar Registration, Active Tracking, Passive Tracking, and Automatic Track Initiation.
*   On-site testing went so well that the system was sold off six months ahead of schedule.
(1989–1990, Tsunami Project; SEI rating = 3)

Member of the Technical Staff II   AeroTech Corporation
                                                        Fort Walton Beach, FL

Technical lead of the Surveillance Group, with thirteen software engineers, on a large-scale realtime system for Japan during the design, code, test, and integration phases of the project.
*   Member of the technical review board setting design, code, and test standards for the project.
(1987–1988, Tsunami Project; SEI rating = 3)

Member of the Technical Staff II   AeroTech Corporation
                                                        Rochester, NY

Site specialist responsible for the testing, debugging, and update of the Weather, Flight Plans, and Manual Inputs applications of a large realtime system for the U. S. and Canada during on-site testing and sell-off of the system.
*   Became familiar with word processor and spreadsheet applications and client/server development environment.
(1986, North Bay Project)

Member of the Technical Staff I   AeroTech Corporation
                                                        Fort Walton Beach, FL

Software engineer responsible for the design, code, test, and integration of the Manual Inputs application of a large realtime system.
*   Obtained extensive experience with both internal and customer presentations.
(1983–1985, North Bay Project)

SYSTEMS
    PC (MS-DOS and Windows), Macintosh, VAX (VMS), NEC MS190D

LANGUAGES
    Fortran, Jovial, Assembly Language, Pascal

AWARDS
    AeroTech Incentive Award–Safe Haven Early Completion Bonus (1996)
    AeroTech Informal Award–Safe Haven Applications Team Key Player (1995)
    AeroTech Incentive Award–UKSafe Early Completion Bonus (1994)
    AeroTech Informal Award–Tsunami Early Completion (1990)
    AeroTech Craftsmanship Award for Excellence in Programming (1986)

EDUCATION
    B.S. Computer Science–University of Florida, Fort Lauderdale (1983).

**Sample Resume:
Seeking Career
Advancement**

NICHOLAS YATES
6970 Deadwood Avenue
Overland Park, Kansas 66202
(913) 394-3723

OBJECTIVE
Administrative Assistant

QUALIFICATIONS SUMMARY
Ambitious, highly energetic, detail-oriented Administrative Assistant with demonstrated expertise in office management, accounting, and operations start-up. Skilled in serving as calm and assertive liaison between management and customers/clients/students. Proficient with Macintosh and IBM compatible computers.

EMPLOYMENT HISTORY

Johnson County Community College, Overland Park, KS   1993–present
Administrative Secretary to Director of Purchasing

- Coordinated overall running of Purchasing Office.
- Composed and typed Purchasing's portion of monthly board packet reports for distribution to executive officers and Administrative Services.
- Created database and maintained records on FileMaker Pro, paid invoices for $461,470 repair pool and $1,176,199 replacement budget.
- Implemented college-wide Full-Time Staffing Chart.
- Tutored students in English and Composition I and II.
- Received cash award for "Extra Efforts" letter.

Good Samaritan Hospital, Cincinnati, OH   1986–1993
Administrative Secretary to Director of Nursing   1991–1993

- Scheduled Task Force meetings and recorded minutes for distribution.
- Composed letters and forms for the Director and 15 Nursing Managers.

Intake Worker; Outpatient Clinic   1989–1991

- Evaluated potential patients for entrance to outpatient clinic.
- Established financial rate, researched insurance information, and arranged appointments.
- Conducted interviews and made financial agreements between obstetrical patients and hospital.

Inpatient Insurance Biller; Business Office   1986–1989

- Billed all secondary insurance; followed up on all medical payments; manned 10-line telephone system.
- Acquired knowledge of all billing, e.g., Commercial, Medicare, Medicaid, Worker's Comp., as "billing floater."

Drs. Appel & Klein, Cincinnati, OH   1984–1985
Office Manager/Medical Assistant

- Established and managed a well-organized, smoothly operating, and efficient podiatry branch office.

EDUCATION
Johnson County Community College, Overland Park, KS   1993–1996

Working toward transfer AA Degree in Journalism (4.0 GPA). Computer courses completed include:
- Microsoft Word
- Microsoft Excel
- Business Desktop Publishing
- Business Graphics on the PC

National Seminars, Inc., Cincinnati, OH   1991–1993
- Powerful Business Writing Skills
- Management Skills for the Secretary
- Dealing with Difficult People
- Powerful Communication and Image Skills

References furnished upon request.

**Sample Resume:
Seeking Career
Advancement**

Kenneth Kelly

222 East Roanoke, #5 Boston, MA 02105 (617)267-7555

Objective	Graphic Artist
Qualifications	Over seven years' experience in digital typesetting, electronic publishing, and computer graphic design, and ten years' experience in traditional graphic arts with a thorough knowledge of the graphic design and print production process.

Graphics Related Skills

- Create clean publication designs with limited resources and achieve high quality standards within tight deadline and budget constraints.
- Proficient user of major computer page-layout, image creation/editing, illustration, and wordprocessing software on both Macintosh and PC (DOS- and Windows-based)platforms including PageMaker, QuarkXPress, Photoshop, Illustrator, Microsoft Word and WordPerfect.
- Maintain working knowledge of graphics-related technologies including system management, scanning, imagesetter output, imposition, trapping, press requirements, and HTML programming for web site development.
- Provide patient, user-friendly computer technical support and software training.

Organizational/Interpersonal Skills

- Manage multiple complex projects and priorities efficiently and delegate when necessary.
- Interact independently and as a team member with all organizational levels.
- Initiate communication and establish successful relationships with clients and co-workers.
- Take initiative to plan, organize, evaluate, follow-up, and resolve problems in a timely manner.
- Keep a positive, flexible attitude and readily adapt to change.

Accomplishments and Awards

- Designed an easy-to-read grant proposal that resulted in an award of $1.5 million to the college.
- Produced educational handbooks that have been used as models for other community colleges.
- Created a unified identity for all department publications including newsletters, stationery, business cards, advertisements, forms, and program manuals; typeset and designed layout for two textbooks.
- Awarded scholarships in graphic design and printing technology and maintained honors level grade point average while employed full-tme.
- Artwork selected for exhibition in the Student Art Show and used for the cover of the College Catalog.

Relevant Employment*

INDEPENDENT CONTRACTOR	
■ **Freelance Graphic Artist/Desktop Publisher**	1996 to present
QUINCY COLLEGE, Quincy, MA	
■ **Graphic Artist/Professional Expert, Computer Lab Technician and Tutor**	1995–1996
COMPOGRAPHICS, INC., Boston, MA (type house and graphic design service)	
■ **Typesetter/Production Artist/Camera Operator**	1994–1995
CCM PUBLICATIONS, INC., Quincy, MA (magazine publisher)	
■ **Paste-up/Production Artist and Bookkeeper**	1993–1994

Education*

QUINCY COLLEGE, Quincy, MA	1993

- Earned Vocational Certificates in Pre-Press: Camera and Stripping, Pre-Press: Digital Photo-compositon (typesetting) and Desktop Publishing (in progress) while pursuing an AA degree in Printing Technology with a General Education focus on Business Management.

* Portfolio review and additional employment/educational information available by appointment.

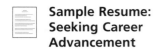 **Sample Resume:
Seeking Career
Advancement**

PROFESSIONAL PROFILE

Richard M. Blakemore
3574 Keswick Road
Baltimore, Maryland 21211
(301) 257-1965

CAREER OBJECTIVE

A position with manufacturing management responsibility offering potential advancement as well as immediate challenge. Am qualified to make a valuable contribution in the following areas: Manufacturing/Operations Manager, Plant Manager, Director of Manufacturing/Operations.

WORK EXPERIENCE

Manufacturing Manager   Bunker Hill Laboratories, Inc.
                                             Baltimore, Maryland

Responsible for all Clinical Reagent and Control Manufacturing including production scheduling and inventory control; computer programming for compounding, inventory, process control, etc.; receipt, storage, and issuance of raw materials, including controlled substances; human blood plasma processing; large and small bulk processing; high speed/volume vial filling; lyophilization (freeze drying); and capping and labeling. Inventory responsibility at Baltimore facility has exceeded $12,800,000 with an average annual production throughput of $15,000,000 at market value.

Recent Major Accomplishments for Bunker Hill Laboratories, Inc.

- Reduced manufacturing work force by 18 percent while exceeding average production volumes by over 29 percent.

- Reduced inventory levels by 32 percent during a period when backorders were also reduced from $1,125,000 to less than $80,000.

- Reduced "problem" production throughout time frame by over 40 percent through improved communications with interfacing departments.

Senior Associate—Assistant Chief Engineer   Coats & Clark, Inc.
Group Engineer—Staff Engineer   Stamford, Connecticut

Responsible for the management of major corporation productivity improvement projects to include directing the activities of 15 to 25 professionals. Cumulative experience includes problem solving, systems design, and installations in the areas of manufacturing, production planning and scheduling, inventory control, material handling, warehousing and distribution, quality control, maintenance, sanitation, and administrative functions. A complete listing of projects is available upon request. Resigned position to reduce travel commitment.

Richard M. Blakemore   Page 2

Production Manager   Stride Rite Corporation
                                           Boston, Massachusetts

Responsible for all production-related functions in a "start-up" operation. Production department expanded from four employees to forty-two employees within the two-year period. Resigned position to accept responsibilities with consulting firm to broaden my experience.

Assistant Facilities Manager—Facilities   Emcee Electronics, Inc.
Supervisor—Facilities Coordinator   New Castle, Delaware

Responsible for maintenance, corporate communication system, contracted security services, contracted janitorial services, capital assets acquisition and inventory, and health and safety programs for a fourteen-building complex with 1,800 employees. Position eliminated during electronics recession when corporation went into receivership. Work force reduced from 1,800 employees to approximately 170 employees.

EDUCATION

Bachelor of Science degree, Engineering, Northeastern University, Boston, Massachusetts.

REFERENCES

Will be provided upon request

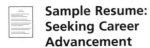 **Sample Resume: Seeking Career Advancement**

MARIA VALDEZ

9090 Camden Place
Miami, Florida 33174
(305) 779-0021

OBJECTIVE:	**Sales Manager**

SUMMARY OF QUALIFICATIONS:
Possess over nine years' diversified and comprehensive experience in wholesale and retail sales, customer relations, purchasing, distribution, and all phases of operating lighting business.

EXPERIENCE AND SKILLS:

Product Knowledge
Broad knowledge of all types of lamps, lighting fixtures, and electrical products for residential and commercial applications. Familiar with nomenclature of electrical and lighting industry.

Communication Skills
Ability to stimulate customers to decision making. Ability to reason with customers and overcome objections. Possess desire and ability to initiate contacts and follow through.

Entrepreneurial Aptitude
Ability to analyze existing services and improve upon same. Imported items for resale for family-run business.

EMPLOYMENT HISTORY

1995–Present
Contractor Sales Representative, Miami, Florida
Facilitate all transactions for contractors. Prepare bids. Compile orders and prepare for delivery. Initiate customer contact and cultivation of customer for future business. Continuous customer service. Instrumental in increasing sales volume during tenure.

Salesperson, Electrical and Lighting Departments
Responsible for customer service and interfacing with vendors. Imparting of knowledge and training to other employees.

1993–1995
Partner, Hummel Lighting, Coral Gables, Florida
Responsible for wholesale purchasing, buying negotiations, direct sales, accounting, and all phases of operating a lighting business. Responsible for generating sales through established customers and through initiation of new customers.

EDUCATION:
Currently attending Miami-Dade Community College, Miami, Florida; working toward A.A. Degree transfer major in Business Administration.

REFERENCES:
Available upon request.

**Sample Resume
Seeking Career
Advancement**

JASON S. WOO
1101 Mesa Verde Drive
San Pedro, California 90731
(213) 549-0045

OBJECTIVE
Biochemistry position with management responsibility

QUALIFICATIONS

TRAINING AND DEVELOPMENT COORDINATION
Developed new employee orientation presentation covering the manufacturing process of clinical chemistry controls

Developed and implemented product flow support system to ensure timely scheduling during all phases of processing

STRATEGIC ACTION
Recommended major procedural change in defibrination of human plasma, resulting in a cost savings of approximately $200,000 per year

Reduced spending significantly on filtration media through more effective filtration techniques; includes clarification, membrane, and ultrafiltration

Developed traceability system for samples used in final product evaluation

Redesigned layout of manufacturing laboratory to more effectively use available space

EMPLOYMENT HISTORY

MANAGER, PILOT SYSTEMS
Bates and Bates Diagnostics, Long Beach, California
Direct manufacturing operations of enzyme immunoassay product line. Responsibilities include formulation, production, material control, and shipping, as well as scheduling. (1995–present)

FORMULATION LABORATORY SUPERVISOR
Directed manufacture of all products, including formulation, filtration and in-process testing. Responsibilities also included purchasing of all raw material and supplies and maintenance of all raw material inventory. (March 1993–Feb. 1995)

FORMULATION BIOCHEMIST
Designed filtration techniques, troubleshooting of process, and product improvement projects. (April 1991–March 1993)

EDUCATION

1993–1996
Courses in Management

Interaction Management (DDI)
Focused Selection Interviewing (Xerox)
Interpersonal Skills in Management (UCI)

GMP Training (GMP Institute)
Employee Training and Development (UCI)
Effective Communications (Cal Poly, Pomona)

1990–1993
Graduate courses in Biological Sciences and Education, California State University, Long Beach

1991
Bachelor of Arts degree, Biological Sciences, California State University, Long Beach

References will be furnished upon request

Sample Resume:
Seeking Career
Advancement

JESUS AGUILAR
9810 Featherhill Drive
La Mirada, California 90638
(213) 694-2272

OBJECTIVE: Manager, Front Desk Operations for a Resort Motel or Hotel

EXPERIENCE

Sales and Marketing Assistant   Holiday Inn
                                                     Anaheim, California

Work with Director of Marketing on budgeting and forecasting for 377-room hotel. Prepare flowcharts and advertising copy. Manage sales efforts with corporation, travel, state, and regional business. Prepare period end projections. Supervise two marketing secretaries. (1995–present)

Meeting Planner   Dorman Investments, Inc.
                                                     Newport Beach, California

Coordinated monthly seminars ranging from small meetings to meetings for groups of 350. Arranged weekend hotel and catering plans for groups. Made prospecting calls. (1994–1995)

Administrative Assistant   Terrace Green Hotel and
                                                     Golf Resort
                                                     Palm Springs, California

Worked with Director of Food and Beverage in a 470-room hotel grossing $17 million yearly. Job included public relations and assisting managers in problem solving, auditing, purchasing, and formatting menus. Worked closely with the Room Sales Department. (1993–1994)

Travel Agent   Sunshine Travel
                                                     Palm Springs, California

Sold cruises, airline tickets, and land tours. Prepared ticket reports. Attended weekly information seminars. (1991–1993)

EDUCATION

Certificate in Hospitality Management, Cypress College, Cypress, California, 1994. Major courses included: Executive Hospitality, Hotel/Motel Front Desk Management, Human Relations in Business, Principles of Advertising, and Information Systems and Computer Programming.

REFERENCES

Available upon request

**Sample Resume
Seeking Career
Advancement**

THERESA ANN VILLASENOR

4055 Huntley Avenue   (801) 595-6072
Salt Lake City, Utah 84116

OBJECTIVE: Director of Nursing/Administrator of Nursing Services

EXPERIENCE:

Registered Nurse   University of Utah Hospital
                                                    Salt Lake City, UT

- Specialized care of patients with various cardiac dysrhythmias and diseases on a 32-bed cardiology/telemetry unit. (September 1995 to Present)

Registered Nurse   St. Luke's Hospital
                                                    Fargo, ND

- **Charge Nurse** responsibilities for a 9-bed AM Admission unit. Care of pre-operative patients and post-procedure short-term stay patients. Served as Unit Educator for this shift. (1993–1995)
- **PM Charge Nurse** on 37-bed Neurosurgery, Urology, Gynecology unit. Supervision of patient care on this evening shift; collaborated with physicians. Responsible for staffing the oncoming shift. (1991–1993)
- **Staff Nurse** involved in primary nursing health care delivery system on 37-bed Neurosurgery, Urology, Gynecology unit. Participated in new employee orientation as a preceptor. (1984–1991)

PROFESSIONAL ACTIVITIES:

- Member of Nursing Policy/Procedure Subcouncil   (1991–1995)
- Member of Nursing Education Council   (1995)
- Member of Urology Joint Practice Committee   (1988–1993)
- Member of task force to develop new medication administration record. Assisted Education Department in development of hysterectomy, prostatectomy, nephrostomy tube patient teaching booklets.   (1994)
- Member of American Urological Association Allied (AUAA)   (1988–1995)
- AUAA Nominating Committee   (1991–1995)

EDUCATION:

St. Luke's School of Nursing, Fargo, ND
Graduated May 1984 with honors
Diploma in Nursing

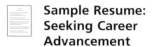

**Sample Resume:
Seeking Career
Advancement**

CLAIRE MARCINKEVICZ, P.E.
6651 East Ocean Avenue, #202
Long Beach, California 90803
(310) 498-2224

CAREER OBJECTIVE

To associate with a progressive civil engineering firm as a project engineer, with opportunity to advance to a project manager position.

EDUCATION

Master of Science in Civil Engineering, Oklahoma State University, December 1987
Bachelor of Science in Civil Engineering, Oklahoma State University, August 1986

PROFESSIONAL AFFILIATIONS

Registered Civil Engineer, State of California, 1992
American Society of Civil Engineering; Women Transport Seminar (WTS)

EXPERIENCE

Project Engineer   Royce-McClary, Inc.
(1992 to Present)   Long Beach, CA

Route 47/Navy Way Interchange, Port of Los Angeles, California

Responsible for preliminary and final design (PSR/Ps&E) of a $40 million project to grade separate Route 47 over future rail access. Responsible for preparation of project report (PR), roadway plans, and coordination with the Port of Los Angeles, Caltrans, and sub-consultants.

Route 66/I-15 Interchange, Rancho Cucamonga, California

Responsible for final design (Ps&E) of a $3.7 million interchange improvement. Designed final geometric plans, profiles, drainage, right-of-way, estimate, and stage construction. Coordinated design documents with sub-consultants, private developers, Caltrans, and the city of Rancho Cucamonga.

Pico Avenue Interchange, Port of Long Beach, California

In charge of preliminary geometric design (PSR) for a $25 million grade separated interchange. Developed more than 20 alternatives for the separation of Harbor scenic drive, Pico Avenue, and local railroads. Performed a leading role in coordination with the Port of Long Beach and sub-consultants.

State Route 91, Riverside, California

Senior engineer responsible for development of conceptual and preliminary design of plans, profiles, ingress/egress locations, CHP enforcement areas, and pavement delineation to accommodate proposed High-Occupancy Vehicles (HOV) within the existing median.

Claire Marcinkevicz   Page 2

Prepared preliminary and final design of on-site drainage plans, which included several channels, new storm drainage system, adjustment, analysis, and extension of several existing culverts throughout the 4.4 miles of Route 91 starting from SR-57 to Lakeview Boulevard.

State Route 71 improvement, Chino Hills, California

Was responsible for preliminary design of plans and profiles for the new ramps, HOV ingress/egress locations, CHP enforcement locations, frontage roads, and new right of way.

State Route 76 improvement, Oceanside, California

Senior design engineer for preliminary design (Ps&E), plan and profile, local intersections of a $47 million, four-lane, six-mile-long expressway.

State Route 78 interchange, San Marcos, California

Senior design engineer for preliminary design of plan and profile for new interchange at Las Posas Road and San Marcos Boulevard.

Senior Design Engineer   Braden Associates
                                                                Los Angeles, CA

As senior design engineer/project engineer, was responsible for preparing project budget estimates, engineering design, hydrology, hydraulics, construction plans, and specifications for many street improvement projects for public agencies such as cities of Rosemead, Agoura Hills, Paramount, Chino, and Moreno Valley. Prepared budget cost estimate for five-year capital improvements for the city of Moreno Valley, California. (1990–1992)

Design Engineer   City of Houston
                                                                Houston, TX

Reviewed structural plans submitted by both in-house and consulting engineers to verify compliance with the appropriate criteria of the building code for the city of Houston. Prepared contract documents and specifications for rehabilitation of existing buildings. Reviewed improvement plans (street, sewer, hydrology, and hydraulics) submitted by private consultants. (1988–1990)

REFERENCES

Available upon request

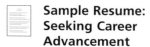

**Sample Resume:
Seeking Career
Advancement**

AUDREE P. LARSON
2801 South Portland Avenue, #108
Bloomington, Minnesota 55404
(612) 998-7088

OBJECTIVE   **Marketing Management Position in the Food Products Industry**

EXPERIENCE   <u>Sensory Coordinator</u>   Pillsbury, Inc.
                                                  Minneapolis, MN
Direct sensory evaluation used for all quality assurance, quality
control, and product development activities. Also plan the daily
sensory evaluation program. Supervise communication of test results
to purchasing, sales, and production scheduling for ingredients
required in manufacturing. Conduct training sessions for new sensory
panelists for participation in triangle difference taste panels and
product preference evaluations. Participate in major meetings with
principle customers and present information on sensory analysis
procedures. (1993 to Present)

<u>Product Development Food Technologist</u>
Formulated new products and improved standards of current
products. Specifications such as flavor, color, pricing, and starch
system were incorporated. Assisted in pilot production runs. Sensory
evaluation along with written and oral skills were used. (1992–1993)

<u>Quality Control Food Technologist</u>
Responsible for the Quality Control Department. Duties included
evaluating specifications of production batches; soluble solids, pH
viscosity, flavor, and appearance for each product manufactured.
Also responsible for evaluating raw ingredients. (1988–1992)

EDUCATION   B.A., University of Wisconsin, Madison (1988)
Major: Foods and Nutrition
Courses studied include calculus, consumer behavior, marketing
management, principles of selling, and business law.

**RELATED
TRAINING**   University Extension, University of Wisconsin, Madison. Short
courses completed: Introduction to Statistical Methods for Sensory
Evaluation of Foods and Sensory Evaluation Update. (1996)

University of Minnesota, Minneapolis. Graduate courses completed:
Sensory Evaluation of Foods and Government Regulations of Foods,
and Research Problems of Foods.

**PROFESSIONAL
AFFILIATIONS**   Phi Upsilon Omicron
Wisconsin Dairy Industries Association
Institute of Food Technologists for Minnesota: Sectional Secretary
    (1996 to Present)
Hospitality Committee (1995–1996)
Membership Committee (1994–1995)

**Sample Resume:
Seeking Career
Advancement**

ANN Y. LIN
2901 Merrimac Avenue
Pittsburgh, Pennsylvania 15222
(412) 391-3801

OBJECTIVE: Position as a Pharmacist in a hospital setting

EDUCATION: **B.S. in Pharmacy**
The School of Pharmacy, Kaohsiung Medical College, Taiwan,
R.O.C. Coursework: Pharmaceutical Chemistry, Organic
Chemistry, General Chemistry, Biochemistry, Pharmacology,
Pharmacy Dispensing Registered Pharmacist in Pennsylvania
License No. RPH 23679. Expiration: November 1998.
Additional classes at Pennsylvania State University, New
Kensington, in business administration and computer science.

**WORK
EXPERIENCE:**   **Pharmacist**   Cook's Pharmacy
                                               Springdale, PA

Duties include filling prescriptions and inventory control. (Part-time:
1993 to Present)

Office Manager   John W. Lin, M.D.
                                               Oakmont, PA

Coordinate office staff, purchase office and medical supplies.
Responsible for accounts payable and accounts receivable. (1988
to Present)

Pharmacy Volunteer   Mercy Hospital
                                               Pittsburgh, PA

Duties included preparing IV and filling prescriptions. (1987 to 1988)

Intern Pharmacist   Pacific Hospital
                                               Pittsburgh, PA

Responsible for filling prescriptions, typing labels, preparing IV and
filled unit dose, preparing control drugs for the operating room and
nurses' stations, and delivering medicine to patients. (1984 to 1987)

Intern Pharmacist   Fisher's Pharmacy
                                               Oakmont, PA

Duties included filling prescriptions and typing labels. (1983 to 1984)

MEMBERSHIP: Pennsylvania Pharmacist Association

REFERENCES: Available upon request.

**Sample Resume:
Seeking Career
Advancement**

MARY M. MALONEY   938 West Arlington, #404, Chicago, Illinois 60614   (312) 738-2137

OBJECTIVE   Marketing/Business Development position in Managed Health Care.

SUMMARY

- 6+ years' marketing experience.
- Demonstrated communication skills and proven ability to manage simultaneous projects effectively.
- Interfaced, negotiated, and secured cooperation with all levels in an organization, including CEOs, administrators, and physicians to achieve outcome-oriented results such as implementing regional strategies, including hospital affiliations, physician integration projects, and payor partnerships.
- Responsible for new business development activities for the following product lines:
  - Multi-Organ Transplant • Cardiothoracic • Colorectal • Gastrointestinal
  - Vascular Surgery • Neurosurgery • Orthopedic Surgery • Cardiology • Primary care

ACHIEVEMENTS

- ✓ Participated as internal contact with McBride & Co. on a strategy and organization redesign project for Humana Healthcare Corporation.
- ✓ Increased hospital's total gross revenue by 15% and direct referral volumes from 6 Illinois counties by over 300%.
- ✓ Secured 15 contracts spanning an extensive catchment area totaling more than 1 million patient lives.
- ✓ Compiled, analyzed and applied real-time market intelligence to Priority Programs, increasing the market penetration rate by over 200%.
- ✓ Serviced broad range of clients: HMOs, medical groups, IPAs, hospitals and health plans, increasing utilization of current contracts by 25%.

BUSINESS EXPERIENCE

Business Development/Managed Care

- Initiated negotiations and presented case rates to HMOs, medical groups, IPAs, hospital risk pools and health plans for Northwestern Physicians and Northwestern University Hospital.
- Recruited primary care physicians from competing medical staffs, redirecting existing referral relationships and increasing physicians' and hospital's total gross revenues.
- Initiated, established, and developed new business relationships, translating productive referral relationships into business systems.

Strategic Planning

- Guided Senior management at Humana Healthcare Corporation in the development and implementation of regional strategies to augment market share.
- Initiated and presented to senior management "partnering" opportunities with payors, community hospitals, medical groups and IPAs.
- Provided corporate with a weekly and monthly assessment of market position.

Marketing

- Developed, executed, and tracked the success of direct mail, cable TV and other promotional campaigns.
- Developed all sales promotional materials, corporate collateral, video and sales presentations.
- Gathered and analyzed market research data for new product introduction and distribution.

MARY M. MALONEY   (page 2)

BUSINESS EXPERIENCE *(cont.)*

Public Relations/Promotion
- Coordinated and executed trade shows, symposiums, conferences, and community events.
- Scheduled speaking engagements for Northwestern University School of Medicine Faculty at community hospitals, medical societies, and other organizations.
- Networked Northwestern's physicians with community physicians at dinner meetings and various events.

Training
- Designed, implemented and evaluated product and sales training programs for distributors, end-users and international sales staff.
- Facilitated sales courses and demonstrations and provided technical support for distributors, international sales staff, and customers.
- Wrote technical documentation for engineering and end-users.

WORK HISTORY

3/1993 - 9/1997	Northwestern University Hospital/Humana Healthcare Corporation, Chicago, Illinois • Client Services Manager • Physician Relations
4/1991 - 1/1993	Evanston Community Foundation Hospitals, Evanston, Illinois • Marketing Liaison
4/1989 - 4/1991	Ameritech, Inc., Evanston, Illinois • Training Manager, telecommunications firm
7/1984 - 5/1988	Southern Geophysical, Co., Houston, Texas • Seismic Data Processor
Prior:	Summer employment with AMOCO Production Company as "Roustabout" Engineer Trainee and Exploration Technologist

EDUCATION
BS Petroleum Engineering, University of Texas at Austin.

COMPUTER SKILLS
- IBM and Macintosh
- Microsoft Office, MS-DOS, Word, Excel
- WordPerfect, Pagemaker, Lotus Notes
- ACT (Automated Contact Tracking System)
- FORTRAN programming

PROFESSIONAL DEVELOPMENT
University of Illinois, Chicago
School of Public Health, Managed Care Programs

PROFESSIONAL AFFILIATIONS
American Marketing Association

7

RESUMES FOR PEOPLE IN TRANSITION

CHANGING CAREERS

Changing careers is not at all unusual in today's world of work. Job statistics indicate that the average person changes careers three to five times during a lifetime. Some people end up in the wrong job or in a field that doesn't interest them. Others find themselves "displaced" by a changing industry. Still others become dissatisfied after a period of time. Dissatisfaction with one's job can stem from many things. Often it lies in the environment surrounding the job, not in the job itself. Environments play an important part in a worker's satisfaction and can influence a person's decision to change careers.

An increasing number of "white collar" workers are now facing displacement as a result of plant closures and downsizing efforts of many companies. If you find yourself in this category of workers, you face a unique challenge. You may need to seek an entry-level position in another industry even though you held a middle management position in your previous job. Although this change may be difficult to cope with, it may be unavoidable. If you find yourself in this situation, strive to communicate your effectiveness on previous jobs and relate how these achievements make you qualified for new positions.

Before beginning your campaign, examine your reasons for changing careers. This subject will not be discussed in depth in this book. However, the bibliography lists some helpful books on the subject of career/life planning.

Let us now assume that you have made the choice to change careers (or have been "pushed" into that choice) and are ready to begin the job search campaign. Before you start your campaign, however, you must take stock of yourself. Chapter 3 discusses matching your skills to job specifications. Go back to that chapter and review your skills inventory. You must have a clear picture of your achievements, skills, and objectives before you can think seriously about marketing yourself, which includes writing your resume.

The resume samples in this chapter are those of people in transition. They reflect actual situations and real experiences—not necessarily ideal experiences. Therefore, they are equally applicable to people who are changing careers by choice as to those facing displacement. Here is a list of the varied careers in transition reflected in the sample resumes in this chapter. The first column lists the individual's present or most recent position; the second column lists the desired position.

Present Position	Position Desired
Word Processor	Office Manager
Office Manager	Industrial Video Producer
Quality Assurance Inspector	Hazardous Materials Specialist
Purchasing Agent/Medical	Purchasing Agent/Electronics
Student Assistant/Job Placement	Personnel Interviewer
Supervisor/Administrator	Nursing Home Administrator
Computer Programmer	Computer Applications Specialist/ Managed Healthcare
School Principal	Personnel Manager
Athletic Trainer	Rehabilitative Physiotherapist
Public/Patient Relations Director	Marketing/Public Relations
Community College Counselor	Dean of Admissions
Graphic Arts Purchasing	Buyer for Manufacturing Company
Welding Supply Manager	Vice President of Sales and Marketing
Federal Agent	Director of Security/Business Operations
Aerospace/Project Manager	Human Resources Manager
Engineer	Trainer
Sales Prepesentative	Paralegal

Study the samples (even though the career objective may be different from yours) to determine how to highlight transferable skills that you can take from one job to another. Some of the examples represent a complete change, such as a secretary/receptionist seeking a position as an assistant manager for a fast food restaurant. College students often acquire much in the way of job skills through on-campus employment. Such is the case of the student assistant in the job placement office seeking a position as a personnel interviewer.

Your primary goal is to emphasize in the resume that even though you used your skills in a completely different work setting, they can be just as valuable in the position you are seeking. For example, the resume for the school administrator seeking a position as personnel manager (see George W. Hertzog) stresses the responsibilities of recruitment, staff development, performance evaluation, and management of operations, all of which have direct applicability to the position of personnel manager. In another sample, a woman (Cynthia Kesaris) who wants to be involved in industrial video production but whose primary work experience was limited to office management has stressed skills acquired in television production classes and in college productions.

Others, such as the community college counselor seeking a position as dean of admissions in a community college (Ruth Sanchez) are not as dramatic, but do represent a transition from one working environment to another using a different set of transferable skills.

SAMPLE RESUMES

The first two sample resumes are Before and After versions. The circled numerals in the Before version refer to the list below, which points out problem areas in the resume. The After version shows the same resume after improvements have been made. The remaining pages in this chapter contain sample resumes for people in transition.

Problem Areas in Maureen L. Smith's Resume

1. No objective is listed in the Before version. Most employers do not want to fit the person to the job; the applicant should know what position he or she is seeking.

2. Only in special cases would the education section come first—for example, if the applicant holds an advanced degree and the education is requisite to the position. Education also should be listed with the most recent accomplishment first.

3. Listing the dates of college attendance calls attention to age.

4. Grade point average should be expressed on a numerical scale (for example, 3.50 on a 4.00 scale).

5. Hobbies and interests are best omitted unless they are directly related to the objective.

6. Work experience more than ten years old is best omitted unless it contains specific skills still requisite to the objective.

**Sample Resume:
Before Version**

MAUREEN L. SMITH
8112 Colima Road, #201
Whittier, California 90605
(213) 234-1809

(1)

EDUCATION: (2)

Chris Business College - 1972
Anaheim, CA

(3) Rio Hondo College - 1991 to Present - B+ Average (4)
Whittier, CA

Currently attending Rio Hondo College on a part-time basis in the Business Administration Curriculum, having completed approximately one full year of college. Recent study includes the Desktop Publishing Course on an IBM-compatible computer utilizing Pagemaker and graphic software.

GOAL: Degree in Business Administration

(5) **HOBBIES/INTERESTS:** Drawing, Watercolor Painting, Petit Point, Graphics

EXPERIENCE:

NORTHROP CORPORATION, July 1991–May 1996

Employed as a Word Processor Specialist in Data Engineering. Formatted manuals, contracts, proposals, specifications, etc., using Microsoft Word. Acted as lead on night shift when lead word processor was on vacation and medical leave, and assisted in training new personnel.

BECHTEL WESTERN POWER CORPORATION, March 1988–July 1991

Employed as Word Processor on the Lexitron and IBM System 6. Formatted technical manuals, specifications, and statistical compositions for a Special Studies Group.

NORTH AMERICAN INFORMATION SERVICES, February 1987–March 1988

Administrative Assistant for the Financial Manager of the Stock and Dividend Department.

(6) Employed from 1972 to 1986 in various positions entailing office experience involving small businesses and a variety of tasks.

 Sample Resume:
After Version

MAUREEN L. SMITH
8112 Colima Road, #201
Whittier, California 90605
(213) 234-1809

OBJECTIVE: Office Manager

SUMMARY OF QUALIFICATIONS:

More than ten years experience in aerospace and engineering environments with increasing responsibilities in word processing, including training and supervision.

EXPERIENCE:

Word Processor Specialist   Northrop Corporation
                                         Anaheim, CA

Format manuals, contracts, proposals, and specifications using Microsoft Word. Act as lead on night shift when needed. Assist in training new personnel. (1991–present)

Word Processor   Bechtel Western Power Corporation
                                         Norwalk, CA

Formatted technical manuals, specifications, and statistical compositions for a special studies group. (1988–1991)

Administrative Assistant   North American Information Services
                                         Pasadena, CA

Office management responsibilities including document authorization, spreadsheet word processing, and scheduling of events. (1987–1988)

EDUCATION:

Currently attending Rio Hondo College. Working toward transfer major in Business Administration. Major courses completed include accounting and business law.

REFERENCES:

Available upon request.

Sample Resume:
Transition

CYNTHIA KESARIS
21790 Redrock Avenue
Tustin, California 92680
(714) 838-4390

OBJECTIVE: Industrial Video and Visual Production and Management

TELEVISION PRODUCTION SKILLS

- Camera Operator/Director of basketball coverage for Fullerton (California) College Athletic Department.
- Camera Operator/Director for Cosmetology Department demonstration for Fullerton (California) College Cosmetology Department.
- Floor Director/Crewperson for "Candidates Night" coverage at the Elks Club on location in Fullerton, California; aired on Channel 32.

WRITING SKILLS

- Developed treatment and working script for a series of 13 half-hour episodes on Career Planning; projected to air on cable television, April, 1997.
- Developed treatment and working script for a 40-minute video program on Juvenile Rights and Responsibilities for the Human Relations Commission of Orange County, California.
- Developed treatment and working script for a series of 13 half-hour episodes on The Traditional Mature Adult Student for the Re-Entry Student Center, to air on cable television in January, 1997

TELEVISION PRODUCTION TECHNICAL SKILLS

Camera Operator
  JVC K4-2700
  Shibaden Rp 1200
JVC RM88U Editor
Production Switcher
Audio Board

Title Camera
16 mm Film Chain
TPT 2500 Titles and
  Generator
Microphones
Portable Light Kits

WORK HISTORY

1993–1996   Robert Marciano, M.D., Inc., Los Angeles, California.
Office manager over front and back office staff and secretary for a pediatric cardiologist in private practice.

1988–1993   Dennis K. Johnson, Poole and Shaw, Architects, San Francisco, California.
Office manager and executive secretary for four partners and four draftspersons.

Cynthia Kesaris

1986–1994   Valley General Hospital/Animal Care Facility, San Pedro, California.
Assistant to the Director of Animal Care, a research facility providing animals
for use in medical experimentation.

1984–1986   Spillman Advertising and Public Relations, Tulsa, Oklahoma.
Media Director for a three-executive company.

EDUCATION

Fullerton College, Fullerton, California, Radio and Television Broadcasting-Production
Emphasis. Degree expected June 1997.

Los Angeles Harbor College, Wilmington, California. Television Production classes. 1993.

Oklahoma School of Accountancy, Tulsa, Oklahoma. Certificate program. 1990.

Tulsa Junior College, Tulsa, Oklahoma. General education. 1987–1988.

REFERENCES

Available upon request.

Sample Resume:
Transition

FRANK ESPINOZA
5055 Caroline Avenue
Lima, Ohio 45804
(216) 423-2761

OBJECTIVE:

Hazardous Materials Specialist

QUALIFICATIONS:

Knowledge of various raw materials and chemicals and their generation of waste streams in manufacturing, agriculture, refining, and chemical production industries. Ability to employ hazardous waste regulation with emphasis in generator compliance, site investigation and remediation, permitting, enforcement, and liability. Excellent written and oral communication skills. Knowledge of manufacturing processes.

EDUCATION:

A.A. Degree, Environmental Hazardous Materials Technology
Lima Technical College, Lima, Ohio. (1997)

Major courses included:
    Waste Stream Generation/Reduction/Treatment
    Health Effects of Hazardous Materials
    Hazardous Waste Management Application
    Safety and Emergency Response

EMPLOYMENT:

Quality Assurance Inspector/Auditor   Sunstrand Corporation
                                         Toledo, Ohio

Perform complex inspection functions in all areas of manufacturing such as casting lay-out, sheet metal flat pattern lay-out, programming, and operating coordinate measuring machines. (1986 to Present)

Transfer Line Inspector   Sundstrand Corporation
                                         Toledo, Ohio

Responsible for inspecting key characteristics at critical monitoring points in a multi-line manufacturing facility. Duties included use of a multitude of inspection devices. (1984–1986)

REFERENCES:

Available upon request

 **Sample Resume: Transition**

WILLIAM G. THOMPSON
871 Pasadena Avenue
Irvine, California 92715
(714) 786-4308
e-mail wgthompson@mci2000.com

OBJECTIVE

Purchasing position within the Electronics Industry.

QUALIFICATIONS

EVALUATION OF ELECTRONIC EQUIPMENT	Evaluated medical equipment as it related to hospital staff and community needs, in addition to financial feasibility. Determined market value of leased equipment related to current technology, reliability, and facility usefulness.
CONTROLLED BIOMEDICAL PROGRAMS	Regulated biomedical service and repair for adherence to hospital requirements and strict regulations set by government regulatory agencies.
ORGANIZATIONAL AND TRAINING SKILLS	Developed and administered training and evaluation programs for medical, administrative, and departmental staff.
ANALYSIS AND STRATEGIC ACTION	Implemented procedure manuals for hospital-wide compliance. Diagnosed and repaired Atari 800 home computer. Recommended major charge procedure revision resulting in approximately $100,000 per year in additional revenue.

SPECIAL TRAINING

EDUCATION	A.M.I. Management Program - Motivational Dynamics Seminar Series. Orange Coast College, Costa Mesa, CA: Full-time student working toward a degree in Industrial Technology; emphasis on Electronics. (January 1995 to present)

Completed courses:

D.C. Theory and Lab	Electronic Drafting
A.C. Theory and Lab	Technical Science
Computer Technology	Mathematics for Electronics

Grade Point Average: 4.0

William G. Thompson   Page 2

EMPLOYMENT HISTORY

PAINTER

ABC Painter, San Diego, California

Painter for a residential painting firm. Experience in brush, spray preparation, and hydro-blasting. (July 1995 to September 1995).

CONSULTANT
PURCHASING

American Medical International, Anaheim, California

Fully responsible for capital equipment requirements in excess of $15 million annually for twelve health care facilities. Active member of the negotiating team for regional equipment and service. Coordinated equipment needs for facility construction, expansion, renovation, or new services. (November 1993 to December 1994).

MANAGER
MATERIALS

American Medical International, Santiago Community Hospital, Santa Ana, California

In complete charge of two departments: Purchasing and Central Service. Responsible for all equipment and supplies from acquisition to disposal. Supervised six employees. Managed shipping, receiving, and storage of supplies. Negotiated supply equipment and service contracts. (July 1986 to October 1993).

REFERENCES

References available upon request.

 **Sample Resume:
Transition**

JONELLE L. LUNDQUIST
1550 Deerpark Drive #127
Kansas City, Kansas 66106
(913) 566-1446

OBJECTIVE

Personnel Interviewer

QUALIFICATIONS

INTERVIEWING | Highly skilled at interviewing both applicants and employers to determine needs and qualifications.

JOB PLACEMENT | Possess ability to follow through on specific placement procedures including use of Pro Search (computerized placement system).

KNOWLEDGE OF JOBS | Extensive knowledge of wide range of positions through personal experience and work experience in a job placement office.

EMPLOYMENT HISTORY

STUDENT ASSISTANT | Job Placement Office, Johnson County Community College, Overland Park, Kansas

Assist in training personnel, on-campus interviewing, and recruiting. Assist vocational students in finding employment on a one-on-one basis. Interview students for positions, and adapt Pro Search to better fit the needs of the office. Reorganized the office and files, organized staff activities, participated in changing policies and procedures. Responsible for employment correspondence and answering multi-line telephones. Take messages, set appointments, place job orders, verify student attendance, and maintain current job openings. Greet students and employers. Proficient in data entry and 10-key by touch. (1995–present)

SECRETARY | Crystal Ice Company, Kansas City, Kansas
Answered telephones, took messages, greeted customers, and set appointments. (1994–1995)

CREW LEADER | United Way, Overland Park, Kansas
Checked and placed volunteers in appropriate positions, greeted public, answered various questions, and handed out schedules. (1993)

EDUCATION

Johnson County Community College, Overland Park, Kansas.
A.A. Degree in Business Management, December 1994.

Major courses included:

Human Relations in Business	Management Communications
Interpersonal Communications	Business Mathematics
Business Law	Accounting 101A
Computerized Accounting	WordPerfect

References available upon request.

Sample Resume:
Transition

DAVID R. KLEIN

210 West Ninety-eighth Street
New York, New York 10034
(212) 744-3966

OBJECTIVE   Nursing Home Administrator

EDUCATION   Currently taking business courses in preparation for Master's in
Business Administration

Graduate work, Columbia University, New York

New York University, Bachelor of Fine Arts in Music

SUMMARY OF   The ability to carry out programs under established policies and
QUALIFICATIONS   command the respect of staff. In addition to problem solving, two
of the important qualities developed from being an administrator,
supervisor, teacher, and customer relations representative are leadership and communication skills.

PROFESSIONAL EXPERIENCE

Supervisor/Administrator - Braille Institute of America
Supervised, screened, hired, and directed the activities of personnel and worked
closely with the staff to ensure the correct and even flow of work, including prop-
erty and grounds. Interviewed student applicants, reviewed case histories, and
assigned study programs and instructors for new students. Coordinated and carried
out adult training program under established policies and student class instruction.

Supervisor - Diabetic Children's Camp, Catskill Park, New York
Coordinated summer youth program. Duties included supervision and training of
50 volunteer teenagers, whose work involved animal care, visitor information, and
food sales.

Supervisor - Poughkeepsie (New York) Juvenile Hall
Supervised boys' section, all activities including work, recreation, special programs,
and inspections.

Teacher - Upstate New York Seventh-Day Adventist Schools
Taught classroom music, piano, and choir in elementary schools. Directed and produced music programs for the schools, including the planning and production of
special holiday programs, recitals, and special emphasis programs.

Volunteer assistant for Kinderkamp and Peps; special summer day school program
for YMCA. Assisted in supervision of all activities for the children.

David R. Klein   -2-

BUSINESS EXPERIENCE

Convention planning, articles for newspaper, program production proposals for campuses of state universities and colleges. New Program Development and Evaluation, New York University.

Assisted with student records (financial and employment), grant and scholarship requests, student registration, and program changes. Office of the Provost, New York University.

Public relations and customer satisfaction being of primary concern, obtained information from customers regarding product complaints. Made decisions as to financial arrangements, (e.g., whether company is responsible to customer for financial remuneration or replacement). Data General Corporation, Boston, Massachusetts.

REFERENCES

Available on request

Sample Resume:
Transition

MARY ANN MILLER   Residence   (404) 451-0190
1434 Monroe Avenue, #204   Business   (404) 568-4411
Atlanta, Georgia 30306   E-mail   mmiller@evernet.com

OBJECTIVE:	A position involving computer applications in the managed health care field.
SOFTWARE & HARDWARE:	COBOL, IMS/VS DB/DC, JCL, CMS/VM, TSO/ISPF, Panvalet, IBM 3090, MVS/XA, Macintosh, PC/DOS, Excel, Lotus 1-2-3, Microsoft Word, dBase III, FoxPro, Windows, MacDraw II, Structured Systems Analysis and Design, Data Modeling, Microsoft Project, SAS, SQL
APPLICATIONS:	Dun & Bradstreet (McCormack & Dodge) General Ledger, Accounts Payable, Bill of Material, Inventory (MRP), Treasury System.

ADMINISTRATION AND ORGANIZATIONAL SKLLS:

- Responsible for contractual service acquistion for use of a Human Resource Information Network system for corporate managers. This involved contractual negotiations, administering purchase process, controlling and maintaining the budget for use of the system.
- Coordinated and directed all quality related activities for an engineering production program, including contacting operations and customer personnel; arranged meetings from start to finish; followed up on action items; acted as a liaison between Quality Assurance and representatives from the customer base.
- Researched, compiled, and prepared data for input to contractual proposals; gathered information through telephone communication, reference materials, and through arranged meetings.
- Responsible for controlling and maintaining the Quality Assurance budget (approx. $400,000) for 3 military programs.

PEOPLE SKILLS:

- Interviewed operations personnel regarding their job duties in order to make productivity improvements.
- Interfaced with vendors, suppliers, customers, and upper management regarding quality matters.
- Provided consulting to customers on the use of software applications and reporting capabilities.
- Coordinated activities between operations, quality and customer personnel.
- Led discussions in meetings to solve people, technical, and resource problems.

TECHNICAL AND ANALYTICAL SKLLS:

- Responsible for developing SAS programs to provide ad hoc reports of statistical and demographic nature for corporate Human Resource Managers. These reports are often of critical and urgent nature; therefore, accuracy and timelines are of significant importance.

MARY ANN MILLER (page 2)

TECHNICAL AND ANALYTICAL SKILLS: (Continued)

- Developed and implemented an Enterprise Information System using EIS PAK, a Microsoft developers package.
- Streamlined the process of importing files from the mainframe to PC Windows applications.
- Responsible for developing Enterprise level head count reports using Excel for the creation of the reports and for the development of graphs.
- Developed and maintained applications using FoxPro.
- Maintained and performed enhancements to Savings Plan Applications using COBOL.
- Team member on General Ledger project to determine technical and functional requirement definitions. Reviewed and evaluated vendor packages; selected Dun & Bradstreet.
- Provided analysis, documentation and recommendations for division's Accounts Payable process which resulted in a restructuring of the Accounts Payable function and achieved a savings of $100,000/year.
- Made modifications to JCLs to support a mainframe billing system.
- Worked independently to perform analysis and documentation of manual and automated interfaces for accounting and financial system. Prepared work flow diagrams using MacDraw II.

EMPLOYMENT HISTORY

1990 to Present	Coca-Cola Enterprises, Inc. Atlanta, GA	Senior Member of Computing Staff
1989-1990	Dun & Bradstreet Software Services, Inc. Atlanta, GA	Quality Planner, Programmer Analyst
1985-1989	Patterson & Dewar Engineers, Inc. Decatur, GA	Quality Engineer

EDUCATION

Georgia State University, Atlanta
Bachelor of Arts Degree in Business Administration, June 1989.
Emphasis in Management Information Systems

Sample Resume:
Transition

GEORGE W. HERTZOG

3027 Webster Avenue, Bronx, New York 10467   (212) 763-9941

OBJECTIVE   Personnel Manager for a medium-sized firm with opportunity to apply experience in a broad spectrum of personnel functions.

EDUCATION   M.S. Degree - Educational Administration, State University of New York, Albany
B.A. Degree - Business Administration, University of Cincinnati.
Additional Graduate Classes - Organizational Behavior and Human Resource Management, Fordham University, Bronx, New York.

EMPLOYMENT
HISTORY

Principal   Westbrook School District
Bronx, New York

- Responsible for recruitment of professional and hourly personnel including interviewing, checking, and evaluating reference information.
- Prepare salary classifications, develop job classifications, and conduct compensation and benefit surveys.
- Monitor turnover and absenteeism, mediate supervisor/employee conflicts, and implement disciplinary actions. Terminate employees involving exit interviews and reports.
- Provide staff development and training programs and organize employee recreational and special activities.
- Management of operations including planning, coordinating, deadline compliance, time management, and program development. (Present)

Assistant Principal   Westbrook School District
Bronx, New York

- Responsible for public relations programs involving heavy public contact and interfacing with supervisors and subordinates.
- Supervised personnel and evaluated performance.
- Managed budget and the utilization of site and equipment.

Sales Representative   Hanover Pharmaceuticals
New Brunswick, New Jersey

- Involved in direct and promotional sales to doctors, hospitals and pharmacies.

RELATED
EXPERIENCE   As a Personnel Technician in the U.S. Army, performed functions of record processing, classification of personnel, and providing individual assistance to recruits.

PERSONAL
VIEWPOINT   Professional and competent recruiting and screening procedures will upgrade and maintain personnel quality, provide acceptable levels of performance, and reduce costly turnover. Receive great satisfaction from observing the results and progress of my actions and influence.

Sample Resume:
Transition

JEFFREY P. LEWIS
4055 Huntley Avenue
Salt Lake City, Utah 84116
(801) 595-6072

OBJECTIVE: Rehabilitative Physiotherapist

EDUCATION: **University of Utah, Salt Lake City, UT**
B.S., Physical Therapy, June, 1997

North Dakota State University, Fargo, ND
B.S., Athletic Training, May, 1994
Minor in Biological Sciences

EXPERIENCE:

Physical Therapy Clinical Affiliations   University of Utah,
Salt Lake City

- Treatment of cerebral palsy, acute care, and other patients in a skilled nursing facility.
- Home health care of head injury patients.
- Participation in spina bifida clinic.
- Treatment planning/follow-up care for post-op anterior cruciate ligament reconstruction; autograft and allograft.
- Rehabilitation treatment planning for I.C.U. patients.
- Demonstrated proper use of therapeutic modalities and documentation of patient care according to policy. (1995–1997)

Athletic Trainer   Red River Sports Medicine Institute
Fargo, ND

- Sport medicine coverage for various sports including ice hockey, basketball, soccer, rodeo, gymnastics. Ages of athletes ranged from five years to college age. (1995)

Head Student Athletic Trainer, NDSU Baseball   North Dakota State University,
Fargo

- On-site injury evaluation, follow-up treatment, and rehabilitation planning along with the incorporation of specific rehabilitation programs tailored to the needs of various playing positions within the sport. (1993–1994)

Assistant Student Athletic Trainer, Wrestling   North Dakota State University,
Fargo

- On-site injury evaluations, follow-up treatment planning, and rehabilitation. (1992–1993)

PROFESSIONAL AFFILIATIONS:
- Member of National Athletic Training Association
- Member of the North Dakota Athletic Trainers Association
- Member of North Dakota Academy of Science

RELATED PROFESSIONAL ACTIVITIES/PUBLICATION
- Publication: "Massage as a Modality in Sports Medicine," *TRAMA,* a medico-legal journal. (In press).
- American Red Cross CPR-BLS Instructor Certified.
- American Red Cross Advanced First Aid and Emergency Care Instructor Certified.
- A.S.U.U. representative for College of Health of University of Utah.
- 1995–96 College of Health Golf Scholarship recipient.
- 1996–97 Continuing Education Physical Therapy Scholarship recipient.
- 1996–97 Gross Anatomy/Cadaver Lab teaching assistant.

Sample Resume:
Transition

TONI ELAINE QUINN
511 Orchid Avenue
Lansing, Michigan 48823
(517) 355-2710

OBJECTIVE
Marketing/Public Relations

SUMMARY OF QUALIFICATIONS
Extensive experience in Hospital Business Development and generating community and physician interest. Programs instituted have added measurably to hospital bottom line. Highly skilled and creative in sales and PR functions. A true self-starter.

EMPLOYMENT

Public/Patient Relations Director
Lansing Regional Medical Center, Lansing, Michigan
- Project long-range marketing goals.
- Conducted survey to assess hospital image and consumer expectations.
- Introduced and managed "Guarantee Service" program, "Courtesy Card" program, "Gold Plan" program, and "Rapid Treatment" program.
- Developed preventive health services, weight control, and nonsmoking units.
- Plan and coordinate dedications, doctor receptions, ground breakings, and open houses.
- Write and release media publications.   (1995 to present)

Director Sales, Group Coordinator Therapist
Bekins Laboratories, Lansing, Michigan
- Coordinated final close of contract on weight control and nonsmoking programs.
- Assigned to the most successful office in the United States.   (1992 to 1995)

Licensed Insurance Agent—Prepaid Dental Plans
National Health Care, Dental Benefits, Charlotte, Michigan
- Cold calls outside sales to industry; marketed dental packages as employee benefits.   (1992)

Licensed Dental Radiology Technician and Dental Assistant
Robert Meyer, D.D.S., Charlotte, Michigan
- Performed technical and dental assistance.   (1989)

EDUCATION
- Michigan State University, East Lansing
  Completed 15 units in Business Administration (1995 to present)
- Lansing Community College (1995) A.A. degree, Liberal Arts

AFFILIATIONS
Hospital Public Relations
- Association of Michigan (HPRA)
- Michigan Society of Patient Representatives (MSPR)
- Eaton County Association of Health Information Officers (ECAHIP)
- Rehabilitation/Civil Rights Committee
- American Society for Hospital Public Relations (ASHPR)
- Community Advisory Council for Lansing Regional Medical Center

REFERENCES
- Furnished upon request.

Sample Resume:
Transition

Ruth M. Sanchez

1101 Sherman Way #201
Sherman Oaks, California 91413
(213) 642-9812

OBJECTIVE

Dean of Admissions and Records

EDUCATION

- UNIVERSITY OF SOUTHERN CALIFORNIA. Sabbatical research in selected coursework in administration and educational psychology. Spring 1995.

- CALIFORNIA STATE UNIVERSITY, Northridge. Master of Science Degree, Counseling, 1987.

- UNIVERSITY OF NEW MEXICO, Master of Arts, Emphasis in Music Supervision, 1983.

- UNIVERSITY OF NEW MEXICO, Bachelor of Arts Degree, Music Education, 1978.

CREDENTIALS

- California Community College Supervisor
- California Community College Counselor
- California Community College Instructor

SPECIAL SKILLS AND ACCOMPLISHMENTS

ADMINISTRATION
  Ability to organize and supervise registration procedures. Familiar with mandated policies of Federal, State, and District guidelines relating to admission and records. Analyzed and evaluated reports from various counseling committees. Acted as chair of high school committee for one year. Plan, schedule, and direct auditions for a performing arts organization of over 140 members. Advise and assist the Board of Directors in development and utilization of a budget of over $350,000. Organize and supervise membership as well as submit and prepare budget items for board approval.

COMPUTER MANAGEMENT
  Extensive experience in the operation and management of computer systems. Able to devise and implement computer management techniques to maximize utilization of computer resources.

Ruth M. Sanchez

RECRUITMENT
>   Coordinated high school recruitment program which involved delegating counselors to various high school career and college days. Established close working relationship with more than 30 high schools and acted as a liaison between them and Los Angeles City College for over a three-year period.

PROGRAM DEVELOPMENT
>   Developed a program for retention of high-risk students, which involves a course on Academic Success and College Survival. Work closely with Admissions and Records when submitting records of completion and statistical data. Responsible for follow-up of probationary as well as F-1 students.

PROFESSIONAL EXPERIENCE

Community College Counselor   *Los Angeles City College*   *Los Angeles, CA*
>   Advise and assist students with academic plans. Teach orientation and college skills classes. Interpret articulation agreements and administrative policies as they relate to students. Involved with daily usage of district-based computer mainframe system for more than two years. (1984–present)

High School Counselor   *Hollywood High School*   *Hollywood, CA*
>   Interviewed, advised, and assisted students with academic plans. Screened, interviewed, and recommended classified staff for employment and promotion. (1981–1984)

LANGUAGE COMPETENCE

Fluent in both oral and written Spanish at an academic level. Knowledge of the culture and linguistics of the Hispanic community.

COMMUNITY SERVICES

- Member of the Los Angeles Master Chorale of Orange County for 12 years.
- Consultant to Grand Jury of Los Angeles County for evaluation of juvenile halls.
- Served as a panel member in the selection of Los Angeles County Sheriff Deputies.

PROFESSIONAL ORGANIZATIONS

- Los Angeles City College Facility Association
- California Teachers Association
- National Education Association
- Facility Association of Community Colleges in California
- California Association of Women Administrators and Counselors
- Student Professional Services Association

References available upon request.

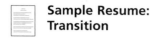

**Sample Resume:
Transition**

NANCY CHENG
8560 Churchill Lane, Apt. 16
Denver, Colorado 80203
(303) 977-8155

OBJECTIVE

To secure a position as a buyer in a large manufacturing company with potential to move up to a management position.

SUMMARY OF QUALIFICATIONS

Seven years' experience in purchasing. Have worked in inside sales, inventory control, and conversion of metals by outside suppliers.

EXPERIENCE

Buyer, Graphic Arts Purchasing   *Martin Marietta*
(1993 to Present)   *Denver, Colorado*

- Prepare and monitor over $7 million in contracts for proposal art and word processing. This includes scheduling and allocation of workload and follow-up of late deliveries or quality problems.
- Negotiate bids for work vended during interface of suppliers and requesters.
- Purchase graphic art supplies including art and printing supplies, printed forms, promotional items, phototypesetting services, and foreign translation.
- Handle and count classified art and word processing work sent to outside vendors.
- Follow up and expedite purchase orders using computerized system.
- Check and approve all contract billing, train back-up material assistants, and prepare miscellaneous reports.

Material Assistant, Graphics Arts Purchasing
(1989 to 1993)

- Purchased business cards, custom framing services, printed forms, art and printing supplies.
- Followed up and expedited purchase orders and provided back-up for buyers.

Material Coordinator   *NBI*
(1985 to 1988)   *Boulder, Colorado*

- Determined from orders and sales forecasts material requirements from mill.
- Placed follow-up and expedited orders including maintaining up-to-date status on minicomputers.
- Aided in forecasting future material requirements and advised sales personnel and customers of current delivery status of orders.
- Interfaced with warehouse and mill personnel to handle material problems and expedite orders.
- Prepared miscellaneous reports and took back-up sales calls.

EDUCATION

June 1994 -   Received A.A. Degree in Business Administration from Denver Community College, Denver, Colorado.

June 1990 -   Received Certificate in Purchasing Management from Westminster Community College, Westminster, Colorado.

References available upon request.

Sample Resume:
Transition

VODELL HAAN
19560 East Cactus Road
Scottsdale, Arizona 85110
(602) 925-9801

OBJECTIVE

Vice President of Sales and Marketing in a major industrial company.
To secure a position in the welding supply industry at the sales and marketing management level.

SUMMARY OF QUALIFICATIONS

Seventeen years experience in the welding supply industry at the distributor, wholesale, and manufacturing levels. Have worked in direct sales, marketing, advertising, and operations as related to inventory control and accounts payable and sales/marketing management.

EXPERIENCE

Manager, Value Protection Products   RGF Industries, Inc. Phoenix, Arizona

- Directed advertising and promotion of new product line.
- Traveled nationally and to Canada to introduce the product line to distributors, manufacturers, and O.E.M.s.
- Produced $120,000 in new business for the Value Protection product line.
- Organized and published distributor and O.E.M. pricing schedules consistent with accepted gross margins.
- Gained acceptance from the Compressed Gas Association for RGF Industries, Inc. based on the Value Protection line.
- Dealt with suppliers; introduced new product lines and expanded old ones.

Sales Manager, Western Region

- Coordinated sales and marketing efforts with six sales territories and five warehouses; Western and Eastern regions.
- Increased sales 18 percent during flat economic times, making best use of the sales territories and advertising.
- Dealt with suppliers; introduced new product lines and expanded old ones.

Marketing Manager

- Coordinated with the advertising department the scheduling, wording, and layout of ads running in the major trade publications.
- Managed the development of two major trade shows (AWS) from conception through participation. Also set up several smaller booth programs.
- Developed, through the advertising department, a new company image with all new packaging, brochures, job racks for distributor locations, and monitored pricing and mailings to distributors. (1994–present)

Vodell Haan (Page 2)

Western Region Sales Manager   PC Cutting Systems
Menonomee Falls, Wisconsin

Was responsible for the sales of thermal cutting machines in seven western states. (1993–1994)

Purchasing Agent   J.C. Peterson Company
Santa Ana, California

Was responsible for purchasing, inventory control, and accounts payable.
During employment there, average inventory turns increased from approximately 3.0 to 5.4, freeing cash for other purposes. (1990–1993)

Sales/Zone Manager   Monroe Equipment Company
Phoenix, Arizona

- Began with inside sales at the Los Angeles retail division; progressed to outside sales in the Orange County territory. Was transferred to Phoenix, Arizona, in 1982 for the Apparatus Manufacturing Division as Zone Manager, working with distributors and end-users. That territory, which included Arizona, Nevada, New Mexico, Colorado, Utah, and El Paso, Texas, increased more than 16 percent each year. In 1984 was again transferred and took over the states of California and Nevada.
- Sales volume increased 43 percent, from $2.8 million to over $4 million, through mid-1983 when the territory was divided. My remaining territory increased another 25 percent through mid-1985.
- Was responsible for the major conversion of Kaiser Steel, Fontana, California, to Monroe apparatus. (1980–1990)

EDUCATION

Seminars and Courses
May 1996   —Senn-Delaney, Leadership Effectiveness Series, four days (34 hours)
February 1996   —AMR, Managing Your Sales Force
January 1996   —Running a Small Business
Bachelor of Science Degree, Business Administration, Arizona State University.

SPECIAL AWARDS

1995—   Co-recipient of "Value Added Award" for the industry at the National Welding Supply Association (NWSA) for advertising and practicing "value added" by the welding distributors.
1995 —   Motivated my sales force to win "East vs. West" sales contest.

REFERENCES

Available upon request.

Sample Resume:
Transition

MICHELLE M. O'BRIEN
Federal Agent
3400 Wisconsin Avenue
Washington, D.C. 20036
(202) 875-5503

OBJECTIVE

Director of Security/Business Operations

QUALIFICATIONS

Experienced Law Enforcement Manager with skills in criminal investigation, public relations, human resource development, recruitment, training, program administration, operational procedures development, security management, surveillance/countersurveillance, interrogations, and financial management. Articulate speaker, skilled instructor, with established national network of professional resources.

RELEVANT PROFESSIONAL EXPERIENCE

MANAGEMENT/INVESTIGATION:
- Managed diverse types of feasibility studies and management surveys
- Directed complex criminal, counter-terrorist, and security clearance investigations
- Developed, prepared, and administered intricate criminal undercover operations
- Planned, controlled, and coordinated multi-agency task forces and inter-jurisdictional investigations
- Managed resources such as travel funds, vehicle fleets, investigation equipment, and undercover operation budgets

PROGRAM DEVELOPMENT/TRAINING:
- Developed and coordinated training programs for State Department Anti-Terrorist Assistance Program, which provides professional skills training to foreign government anti-terrorist security and police forces
- Designed three-day Hostage Negotiation Course, Instructor's Guide, and Training Manual required for U.S. State Department security officers preparing for overseas duty
- Designed and administered classroom and practical training in dignitary protection, international terrorism, anti-terrorist defensive driving techniques, threat recognition and detection, security management, and counter-surveillance for selected foreign and domestic police

SECURITY/DIGNITARY PROTECTION:
- Annually served on foreign dignitary protective details during the United Nations General Assembly, New York
- Served as Lead Advance Agent for the protective detail on the President of the European Community during the Economic Summit of Industrialized Nations, Houston, 1990, coordinating with White House Staff, foreign governments, federal and local law enforcement agencies

Michelle M. O'Brien   page 2

- Member of U.S. Secretary of State Protective Detail, foreign and domestic venues

COMMUNICATION:
- Prepared and presented complex security briefings to senior State Department officials, local police, and corporate security officials
- Promoted State Department and law enforcement programs through networking and speaking at major conferences
- Successfully negotiated peaceful resolutions for crisis/hostage situations
- Conducted news conferences and public relations activities

CAREER HISTORY

U.S. DEPT. OF STATE/BUREAU OF DIPLOMATIC SECURITY: SPECIAL AGENT
1990–Present: Los Angeles Field Office, Houston Field Office, Washington, D.C., Training Divisions.
Program Manager; Instructor; Counter-Terrorist Driving Instructor; Criminal and Personnel Security Investigations; Liaison with foreign consulates, federal, and local law enforcement; Protective Security, foreign and domestic venues

ARLINGTON POLICE DEPARTMENT: POLICE OFFICER, Arlington, VA
1979–1990:   Primary Hostage Negotiator; Media Relations Management; Vice/Narcotics/Criminal Intelligence Investigator; Sensitive Intelligence Investigations; Organized Crime and Subversive Groups; Vice and Narcotics including Undercover Operative; Detective, Sex Crimes; Expert Witness; Patrol Officer

ALEXANDRIA POLICE DEPARTMENT: POLICE OFFICER, Alexandria, VA
1977–1979:   Crime Prevention/Community Relations: Created community-based police programs, designed and presented crime prevention programs

SPECIALIZED TRAINING/AWARDS

Anti-Terrorist Defensive Driving Instructor
Community Mediation—Federal Mediation Services
Dale Carnegie School of Public Speaking
Department of State Spanish Language Training
Instructional Methods for Trainers—California State University
California Commission on Peace Office Standards and Training—Basic, Intermediate, and Advanced Certificates
Recipient Meritorious Service Award—State Department
Affiliation with many professional organizations

EDUCATION

- Post-graduate—Clinical Psychology—Georgetown University, Washington, D.C.
- B.A. Business Management—University of Maryland, College Park
- A.A. Administration of Justice—Prince George's Community College, Largo, MD

**Sample Resume:
Transition**

RUTH SILVERMAN
1909 Cherry Blossom Lane
Seattle, Washington 98094

Home Phone: (206) 511-2840
Work Phone: (206) 566-6000

OBJECTIVE: Human Resources Manager

SUMMARY: Human Resources professional with 14 years experience in a variety of HR functions. Proven ability to manage multiple projects and work with all levels to anticipate problems and meet deadlines. Word processing experience. Strong communication and facilitation skills.

EXPERIENCE: THE BOEING COMPANY

Seattle, Washington
1984–Present

HR Consultant

- Team Leader for Morale Team which provides communication link between employees and the Executive, Transition, Phase Down, and People Teams. The team also develops and implements processes to ensure discussion of Employee Opinion Survey issues.

- Co-Team Leader for People Team which implements actions to ensure a successful transition of employees affected by plant closure. Responsibilities include liaison to site executives and transition teams.

- Consult with executive and division leadership to improve the nomination process for management/executive development programs. Ensure alignment between company goals and employee development.

- Design and implement outplacement programs for employees scheduled for layoff, which include: counseling, job resource workshops, and resume preparation. Involves interface with staffing, employee relations, and benefits specialists.

- Provide career counseling to employees and assist in the development of career decelopment programs.

Project Management

- Administer site and division mentoring program by initiating and implementing process, communicating with participants, scheduling training, and tracking evaluations.

- Develop procedures and guidelines for cascaded training programs. 800 managers completed training in Total Quality Leadership in 85 classes conducted during a 12-month period. Activities also included tracking of participant feedback surveys as well as tracking all costs for 15 separate organizations. Record keeping saved the company $4,000 in invoicing errors.

- Administer Education Reimbursement Program for the site.

- Design organizational surveys for evaluation of job rotation programs for high potential managers. Conduct internal customer interviews and data analysis.

Ruth Silverman

Organization Development

- Develop business strategies which integrate this organization with the site's key profit centers.

- Consult to sector level management.

- Strategic development/troubleshooting and implementation of HR department cmi process improvements in the areas of internal and customer communicaiton, reduction of cycle time, and team building.

- Participate in "Process Work" training to provide employees with negotiation skills for conflict resolution.

Instruction/Facilitation

- Instructor for vendor-developed courses, including: leadership, presentation/communication, conflict resolution, teaming valuing diversity, and empowering the workforce. Consistently rated as Outstanding by workshop participants.

- Coach managers on-the-job to strategically apply leadership concepts and techniques.

- Facilitate process improvement teams on request.

COMMUNITY SERVICE:

- Represent Boeing as member of the Board of Directors for the County Academic Decathlon (CAD). Administer the Boeing Scholarship Program. Serve as corresponding secretary for the Board.

CERTIFICATIONS AND AWARDS:

- Boeing Superior Performance Award, 1994.

- Development Dimensions International: Techniques for an Empowered Workforce, 1994.

- Blessing/White: Managing Personal Growth, 1992.

- Shipley Associates: Professional Presentations, 1990.

EDUCATION:

Bachelor of Arts, *Magna Cum Laude*

University of Washington, Seattle

Completed 30 graduate units in Elementary Education

Seattle University, Seattle

Sample Resume:
Transition

RICHARD S. HESS
555 Wedge Drive
Reston, Virginia 22090
(703)264-1142

OBJECTIVE

Training position in a computer environment.

SUMMARY OF QUALIFICATIONS

A combination of eight years experience in various training and computer-related activities including Computer-Based Instruction (CBI), Computer-Aided Manufacturing (CAM) training, local area network (LAN) maintenance, and C and dBase code generation.

SUMMARY OF SKILLS

Training. Reviewed Air Force radio operator course and generated necessary training materials. Developed computer-based lessons to train operators on maintaining air defense equipment. Trained operators on using UNIX-based CAM system. Instructed youths on fundamentals of baseball; tutored children in mathematics.

Computer. Operated CAM system. Obtained both PC and Macintosh experience. Maintained PC-based Novell LANs. Generated digital signal processor algoithm code, in C. Programmed in Pascal, FORTRAN, Basic, dBase, and assembly languages.

PROFESSIONAL EXPERIENCE

Computer-Based Instructional Designer   Hughes Aircraft Co.
Reston, VA

Design and development of CBI lessons for maintenance of a foreign air defense system (1993–present).
- Researched operation and maintenance of air defense equipment.
- Developed computer-based lessons in Authorware Professional on a Macintosh platform to train operators on maintenance procedures for air defense equipment.
- Reviewed computer-based lessons for quality, instructional soundness, and correct operation.
- Received program-wide incentive bonuses for achieving schedule milestones.

Manufacturing Automation Engineer   Hughes Aircraft Co.
Reston, Va

Assessment, procurement, and maintenance of various computer and manufacturing improvement systems for company CAM, data transfer, and production control needs (1990–1993).
- Researched, evaluated, and purchased various automated manufacturing systems.
- Saved $9,500 by partially automating mechanical fabrication facility.
- Trained operators extensively on UNIX-based CAM system.
- Acted as liaison between company manufacturing and engineering areas including facilities throughout the United States.
- Maintained several PC-based Novell local area networks.
- Developed program code for dBase III+ production control and CAM systems.
- Obtained "New Quality Technology" instruction on Taguchi methodologies, statistical design of experiments theory, and variability reduction techniques.

Richard S. Hess (page 2)

Software and Systems Engineer
Raytheon Company
Lexington, MA

- Generated digital signal processor algorithm code in C.
- Obtained satellite experience including test support, risk analysis, software specification development, and contract proposal writing.
- Obtained U. S. government secret clearance (1986–1990).

Research Assistant
University of Notre Dame
Notre Dame, IN

- Studied basic concepts of fiber optic technology (1985–1986).

Associate Engineer
Hughes Aircraft Co.
Reston, VA

- Developed and tested software and composed technical documents (1984–1985).

EDUCATION:

University of Maryland
- Courses taken in Robtoics, Computer Architecture, and Pascal (1987–1988).

University of Notre Dame
- BS in Electrical Engineering with Computer Science concentration (1986).

University of Maryland
- Program for High School Scholars (1982).

Harvard University
- Secondary School Summer Program (Calculus, Computer Science) (1981).

HONORS/ACTIVITIES:

- Member of IEEE (Institute of Electrical and Electronics, Engineers) (1986–1991).
- Designated Notre Dame Scholar upon admission (1982).
- Bausch & Lomb Honorary Science Award (1982).

SPECIAL SKILLS/INTERESTS:

- Programming in C, Pascal, FORTRAN, Basic, dBase, and assembly languages.
- Coaching sports.
- Tutoring math and computer science.
- Teaching and counseling.

Sample Resume:
Transition

JOHN WEST
63 Rio Dell Drive
Novato, California 94949
415-897-7518

OBJECTIVE: Paralegal/Legal Assistant

SKILLS:
- Computer literate with all major applications.
- Excellent writing, communication and research skills.
- Reading and writing fluency in Spanish.
- Experienced with civil litigation wills, trusts and bankruptices.
- Self starter, people oriented, highly motivated, team worker.

WORK EXPERIENCE

1997–Present   **Paralegal.** *Associated Paralegal Services, Novato, CA*
File court documents, type legal forms, process serving, legal research, customer relations, advertising, and marketing.

1994–1997   **Paralegal.** *Wollborg/Michelson Personnel Service, Inc. San Rafael, CA.*
Drafted complaints, answers and motions; performed legal research; located, interviewed and obtained witness statements; organized and analyzed client documents.

1993–1994   **Telemarketing Specialist.** *Ambassador Technologies, Tiburon, CA*
Led company in sales, trained new staff, obtained leads, responded to software problems, installed, maintained and upgraded computer software and hardware, performed troubleshooting tasks.

1992   **Collection Agent.** *California Service Bureau, San Rafael, CA.*
Debt collection, systems training, supervision, and managerial duties.

VOLUNTEER WORK

Counselor of a youth summer camp program. Organized daily activities and was responsible for 18 youths ages 12 to 17. Volunteered for the Marin County Health Department's Tobacco Education Program.

EDUCATION

1997   **B.A. in Management** with concentration in Marketing.
1995   **A.A. in Liberal Arts,** Honor Roll 1993–1994.
College of Marin, Kentfield, CA.

ACTIVITIES/INTERESTS

Member, Sonoma State University Marketing Association.
Actively committed in church and involved with youth activities.

8 RESUMES FOR SPECIAL PURPOSES

The guidelines for writing an effective resume are essentially the same for all types of workers. Some people, however, may have to pay special attention to the way they present the facts in their resumes. These people include displaced workers, foreign-born individuals, veterans, people with disabilities, people returning to work after an absence of years, and older workers. Because each of these groups has unique concerns, each will be discussed separately.

DISPLACED WORKERS

Massive reorganization efforts in American industry have resulted in large numbers of displaced workers. White collar defense workers were especially hard hit during the economic downturn of the early 1990s. As a result, many highly trained specialists and engineers have been forced to seek new employment in a related industry, to become self-employed, or to change careers entirely. The sample resume for Joseph P. Flores is a model for an aerospace worker transitioning to another industry.

FOREIGN-BORN INDIVIDUALS

If you are foreign-born, probably the first point you should consider is how to use your native language to your advantage. You may have to highlight for the employer the advantages of being able to speak more than one language. For example, your ability to translate written documents from one language to another can be a great asset and should be stated on the resume. In other situations the employer may need to be convinced that you are fluent enough in English to handle the job. In that case, you will have to give examples that substantiate your capabilities. You will especially want to point out your previous jobs that required oral communication. This is recommended for all foreign-born applicants.

When discussing education on the resume, be sure to highlight any training you have had in the English language and where you received it. If the education took place outside of the United States, you may want to clarify the level of your education and indicate equivalencies. When describing work experience, be sure to describe what you did in terms that indicate clear understanding of the English language; be sure the resume is grammatically correct. Employers feel they take more of a risk with people speaking limited English, so you need to prove that the risk will be minimal. The resume of Ashraf Shah in this chapter illustrates the above points.

VETERANS

You will want to capitalize on the fact that you are a veteran. First of all, clearly state in your resume how long you served, the branch in which you served, and your rank on discharge. Pay particular attention to the training you received, your special recognitions, and achievements. Use terms the employer understands so as to bridge the gap between military and civilian vocabulary. Try to equate all the specialized and technical training you received in the service to formal education. Because the training is concentrated, be sure to state your experience in terms of transferable skills. For example, if you have been trained in avionics communications (see the resume of Leroy W. Smith), your knowledge of electronics can carry over to many technical fields.

PEOPLE WITH DISABILITIES

Recent federal and state legislation has done a great deal to improve and equalize job opportunities for people with disabilities. Although legislation has been enacted to protect their civil rights, the problem of awareness and enforcement remains. Enforcement thrust upon the employer prior to awareness is not always effective. First of all, the employer must be made aware of facts concerning an applicant's abilities and disabilities. Employers need to know that most people with disabilities can do most jobs, given the proper training and possibly assistive devices to do the job.

Before you can sell yourself to an employer, you need to be motivated and believe in yourself. But you should not apply for a job for which you are not qualified just because you are in a "protected" category. Start with your abilities and proceed as you would with any resume. Don't concentrate on your disability. If your disability does not interfere with your ability to perform the job, there is no reason to mention it. If you are in a wheelchair, you may want to determine prior to the interview whether the work site will accommodate a wheelchair. If you think the information regarding your disability may be useful to an employer, include it in your cover letter.

Employers who are working under affirmative action concepts will want to know if you have a disability or are among the group protected by federal and state legislation (disabled, minority, veteran, etc.). If, however, you believe that some of this information is unnecessary, you are under no obligation, according to the law, to include it. A sample cover letter for a person with a disability is included in Chapter 9. The resume for a person who has a disability is designed to sell skills and achievements just like any other resume. In summary, be persuasive and concentrate on your ability to perform the tasks necessary for the job.

PEOPLE RETURNING TO WORK

More than ever before, men and women are being given guidance and assistance in returning to work outside the home. Various community groups, YWCAs and YMCAs, colleges, and universities offer programs designed to assist those returning to work. The first chapter of this book discusses functional and transferable skills. The underlying premise here is that returning workers must translate their skills to the work world. It is extremely important that the job seeker take inventory of his or her skills, many of which will not have been acquired on a "paid" job.

The functional and analytical resume styles work best for the person returning to work. Emphasize recent education and any work experience, and point out any volunteer activities you were involved in during the gap in work experience. Give personal information only if you believe it will enhance your chances of getting the job.

Some examples of situations from which to draw transferable skills include:

- Church Groups: Organized a positive singles group and served as its first chairperson.
- P.T.A.: Was elected president of the P.T.A. unanimously for two consecutive years.
- Fund-Raising Events: As ways and means chairperson of P.T.A., raised $5,000 in one day.
- Political Campaigns: Was campaign manager for a candidate who made a successful bid for city council.
- United Way and Other Types of Drives: Achieved 90 percent participation as Cancer Crusade Chairperson for the city of Atwood.
- Philanthropic and Educational Associations: Selected 25 civic leaders, representing City Hall, schools, businesses, and senior citizens, as members of planning committee for Culver City's 50th Birthday Celebration. Organized dinner and entertainment arrangements for 500 people.

The list could go on and on. The resume sample for people returning to work includes volunteer accomplishments. Go back to Chapter 3 for lists of words to help you describe your involvements in organizations. All too often, the returning-to-work job seeker dismisses these achievements as "only volunteer work." These skills indeed have their equivalencies in the business world!

OLDER WORKERS

Little or no consensus exists as to the age at which a worker is referred to as "older." For that reason, the age range is left to the discretion of the reader. The older worker may be transferring skills from one company to another, or planning an entirely new "retirement" career. A job change should not be difficult for the older worker if it is upward movement and based on achievement. The change does not seem to pose as much of a problem in the professions and in the public work sector as it does in business and industry.

Here again, a persuasive approach must be taken. Do not give evidence of age in the resume or cover letter. Use a functional resume to sell your skills, and emphasize recent education and work experience. You should emphasize what you did, not when you did it. You need to think of your age as an asset, not as a barrier to what you want. Use a "Summary of

Qualifications" section directly under the objective, to provide an overall picture of your qualifications. For example:

> Eighteen years' experience in the sale of consumer goods, with consistent record of promotion and accomplishment. Hired, trained, and supervised sales staff numbering up to 85 for home and branch office operation. Devised and supervised sales promotion and market research projects; originated advertising programs in conjunction with advertising agency. Experienced in overall management of sales and related functions.

Go back and review all your achievements on your various jobs. This is not the time to be modest. You want the employer to know he or she is buying a certain expertise that comes only from experience. For example, you will want to emphasize points like these:

- Saved the company $2 million in computer downtime over a period of ten years.
- Through my efforts of negotiation, was able to avoid a major strike by production workers.
- Increased sales and profits by 30 percent without an increase in overhead.

All resume writers can use these techniques, and they are especially useful for the older people who recently have found themselves thrust into the job market. They will want to go back and take inventory of all voluntary activities as well as work experience and highlight the transferable skills. The new retirement age along with increased life expectancy will make job seeking after age forty common on the labor market scene.

Sample Resume:
Displaced Worker

JOSEPH P. FLORES
540 Sea Cliff Drive #10
Newport Beach, California, 92660
(714) 759-7514

OBJECTIVE: Electronics Technician

SUMMARY OF   Electronics Communications Supervisor and Technician with over 16
QUALIFICATIONS   years experience operating and maintaining sophisticated electronics
                  equipment.

PROFESSIONAL HISTORY

1992 to Present   ELECTRONICS TECHNICIAN, McDonnell Douglas, Huntington
                  Beach, CA
                  Install sensitive electronic communications equipment and various
                  associated components.

                  TECHNICAL SERGEANT, United States Air Force,
                  1972 to 1992 Offutt AFB, Nebraska:

1991 to 1994   SUPERVISOR, COMMUNICATIONS TECHNICIAN
                  Performed Command Technical Control using test procedures and
                  equipment. Supervised operations, maintenance, and troubleshooting
                  of all command and control communications systems to include:

                  • SHF Spred and UHF wide spectrum satellite systems.

                  • Frequency division and time division multiplexer and electronic
                    switchboard.

                  • Supervisor of testing and acceptance of UHF satellite and LF/VLF
                    systems.

1990 to 1991   TECHNICAL WRITER/SYSTEMS ACCEPTANCE TESTER
                  Performed environmental testing of aircraft and communications
                  systems.

1983 to 1990   DIGITAL DATA SHOP SUPERVISOR AND TECHNICIAN
                  Assisted contractors with isolation interfacing problems on installation
                  of the LF/VLF and the UHF satellite systems.

EDUCATION (MILITARY AND CIVILIAN)
                  OJT Trainer Orientation—1994
                  USAF Effective Writing—1991
                  Technical Control Element (E-4B)—1991
                  AN/USC-28 (V) Satellite Communications System, Magnavox
                      Advanced Products and Systems—1990
                  Noncommissioned Officer Academy—1989
                  616A System Organizational Inflight Maintenance—1989
                  Air Force Satellite Communications (AFSAT)—1988
                  E4B Systems Interface Operator Training Course—1987
                  (SAC) Airborn Command Post Communications Equipment Repair—1982
                  Currently working toward A.A. transfer major in Electrical Engineering
                      at Orange Coast College, Costa Mesa, CA

REFERENCES: Available upon request

Sample Resume:
Foreign-Born

ASHRAF SHAH
7022 North Broadway
Raleigh, North Carolina 27608
(919) 737-3741

CAREER OBJECTIVE	A position in optical communication systems, high energy lasers, or other physicist position.
EDUCATION	North Carolina State University, Raleigh B.S. Physics expected June 1998
	Coursework includes: Calculus for Science and Engineering; Advanced Classical Mechanics of Physics; Electricity and Magnetism; Quantum Mechanics; Plasma Physics; Pascal Programming.
HONORS AND ACTIVITIES	Dean's Honor List; Society of Physics Students—Sigma Pi Sigma; Treasurer dormitory floor; Intramural Football; Intramural Basketball; Intramural Softball.

WORK EXPERIENCE

Warehouse Assistant   1993–present
Reed Furniture Warehouse
Raleigh, NC

Organized furniture stock. Prepared furniture for delivery. Assisted in delivery of furniture. Assisted in building rooms that expanded office space. Increased storage area by assisting in constructing furniture racks. Developed communication and organization skills as well as ability to work cooperatively with others. Earned 30 percent of college expenses.

Cafeteria Worker   1993–1995
N.C.S.U. Student Union
Raleigh, NC

Assisted in kitchen, maintained dining area. Responsible for produce pickup. Improved kitchen working conditions.

BACKGROUND INFORMATION	U.S. citizen. Enjoy jazz music, viewing sports, participating in sports, organizing, analyzing.
REFERENCES	Will be furnished upon request.

Sample Resume:
Veteran

LEROY W. SMITH

2740 Olive Avenue, Fresno, California 93728   (209) 829-9900

OBJECTIVE: Electronics Technician

EXPERIENCE: TELONIC INC., 683 Sundial Way, Fresno, California

Training
and Methods
Analysis

Responsible for upgrading assembly quality to meet MIL Spec on an eight-person assembly line. Inspected all kits prior to turning over to assembly workers for completion. Analyzed assembly problems of individual workers, devised solutions, and trained personnel, as needed, in new methods. Inspected all output from production line prior to quality assurance. This raised production line quality substantially. When required, functioned as lead, assigning kits to production personnel, logging them in and out. Did rework and continuity checks as required. (6/96–9/97)

Unit
Training
Manager

DEPARTMENT OF DEFENSE - UNITED STATES AIR FORCE
Responsible for all training in Civil Engineering Squadron while stationed at Chanute Air Force Base, Rantoul, Illinois. Coordinated required training through other agencies both on base and off base as necessary for both officers and enlisted personnel. Inspected all training records in the squadron on a regular schedule. Supervised the upgrade training of all personnel in training status. (6/81–7/93)

Avionics
Communications
Specialist

DEPARTMENT OF DEFENSE - UNITED STATES AIR FORCE
Using my electronics knowledge, maintained all avionics communications equipment, including radios, intercommunications systems, auxiliary receivers, and antennas. Using approved troubleshooting techniques and technical orders, repaired equipment to the component level. This required the use of common and specialized test equipment and tools, both on board the aircraft and in the repair shop. Removed and installed avionics communication equipment on F4, F5, T33, T39, and other transient aircraft as required. Inspected, tested, and repaired emergency hand-held communication equipment. When on 30-day temporary duty to Okinawa, was responsible for all avionics equipment, including navigational aids and instruments on all aircraft assigned to the Aggressor Squadron. (5/87–6/91)

EDUCATION: FRESNO CITY COLLEGE, Fresno, California.
A.A. Degree, Electronics Technical, June 1989. Major courses included: AC & DC Circuits, Computer Technology, Electronic Construction, Electronic Instruments, Electronic Drafting, and Computer Aided Design.

UNITED STATES AIR FORCE
Courses in Basic Electronics including AC and DC circuitry, Avionics Communications, Supervisor Course on Management Techniques, Technical Instructor Course, and On-the-Job Training Administrator course.

Sample Resume: Person Returning to Work

BRENDA PLATT
5340 Carnation Lane
Costa Mesa, California 92626

OBJECTIVE:

Convention and Banquet Coordinator/Salesperson

SUMMARY OF QUALIFICATIONS:

SUPERVISION   Experienced hostess and coordinator for wedding receptions and dinner parties which included supervision of a work crew in the set-up, preparation, and presentation of food, as well as clean-up and general operation of the function.

COORDINATION   As president of PTA, was responsible for 24 committees and 50 chairpersons, as well as a variety of social functions and fundraisers for the benefit of the school, children, teachers, and parents.

SALES   As an independent sales representative, initiated contacts, made appointments, planned programs, presented programs, closed sales, and followed through with delivery of merchandise.

As a real estate broker, advertised and promoted listings, made appointments with prospects, negotiated contracts, procured financing, and completed details of processing and closing.

EMPLOYMENT:

1995 to Present   Supervisor/Hostess
The Golden Carrot, Santa Ana, CA

1991–1993   Sales Representative
Tupperware, Inc., Santa Ana, CA

1988–1990   Real Estate Broker
Century 21 Realtors, San Diego, CA

VOLUNTEER ACTIVITIES:

1994–1995   PTA President
Our Savior's Lutheran Church School, Costa Mesa, CA

EDUCATION:

Orange Coast College, Costa Mesa. Working toward transfer degree in Business Administration.

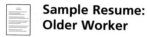

**Sample Resume:
Older Worker**

CHARLES GOMBERG

22814 Admiralty Way
Bellevue, Washington 98204
(206) 970-6353

OBJECTIVE: CREDIT MANAGER

Seeking a challenging opportunity as a Credit Manager. Can assume complete responsibility for a medium-sized organization.

SUMMARY OF QUALIFICATIONS

Possess 18 years' successful experience in Credit/Collection operations and Credit/Collection of management environments. Background includes the following categories:

Extensive experience in credit analysis and collection functions . . . Credit department organization/reorganization . . . Development and implementation of sound and profitable credit policies and procedures . . . Financial analysis and credit line establishment . . . Involvement with corporate attorneys included assisting in the preparation of data against customers in default . . . Possess thorough knowledge of various mechanics and lien laws for several states as well as Uniform Commercial Code Functions . . . Familiar with all aspects of accounting and office management functions.

PROFESSIONAL EXPERIENCE

Regional Credit Manager

Diamond Industries
Seattle, Washington

Currently serving as a Regional Credit Manager for an international leader in refining and fabricating precious metals. Responsible for all of the credit approval and collection activity in the territory of the fourteen western states including Alaska and Hawaii. Basic duties and responsibilities include: to investigate all prospective customers; to assign or revise credit limits to new and existing customers; to contact customers who become past due and arrange repayment of their obligations. Operate a computer terminal that is linked directly with the main computer in New Jersey; this allows me to receive an instant "read out" of what the customer owes at any given time.

Have a credit limit approval authority up to $100,000 on any given account and recommend to the controller any credit limit amount above $100,000. Coordinate credit extension and collection efforts with other regional credit managers within the company.

Resume of Charles Gomberg

PROFESSIONAL EXPERIENCE (Continued)

Assistant Credit Manager

Stan Tennell and Company
Seattle, Washington

Responsible for handling all of the functions within the credit department; had approximately 400 accounts with a total of $5,000,000 in receivables per month. The general territory was Washington, but also had accounts in Northern California, Oregon, Arizona, Utah, and Colorado.

Assistant Credit Manager

James-Miller Contracting
Belleview, Washington

Duties included performing credit investigation, credit analysis, and credit approval functions. Was primarily involved with performing and coordinating all collection activities relative to delinquent accounts. Worked closely with attorneys relative to gathering data for clients seriously in default.

Credit Manager

Gitten Industries
Tacoma, Washington

Duties included performing credit investigation/analysis and approval functions. Established credit lines, controlled receivables, coordinated collections, solved problems relative to credits and billings, and edited and balanced receivable aging reports. Was initially employed as the Assistant Corporate Credit Sales Director and was promoted to a position of increased responsibility.

PRIOR

Served in credit and collection capacities for General Electric Credit Corporation, Thermador Company, and Whirlpool Corporation.

EDUCATION

University of Portland, Portland, Oregon
Liberal Arts Coursework, 40 units

Shoreline Community College, Seattle, Washington
Mid-Management Coursework, 12 units

Building Materials Dealer Credit Association
(Sponsored by General Electric Company)
Mechanics Lien Laws
Credit/Collection Course

9 | THE COVER LETTER

SELLING YOURSELF

The cover letter or letter of application introduces you and asks for an interview and, with very few exceptions, should accompany a resume. The cover letter creates attention and leads the reader to the resume. Many times an employer will offer an interview on the basis of an outstanding cover letter. On the other hand, a cover letter that contains poor grammar or typographical errors may cause the employer to eliminate the applicant from consideration. *Do not minimize the importance of a good cover letter.*

The Opening Paragraph

Think of the cover letter as a "sales" letter. The first or opening paragraph should be designed to create attention. Some openings designed to create attention are: summary, name, request, and question. All four of these sample openings are represented in the sample cover letters on the following pages.

The Middle Paragraph(s)

The middle paragraph(s) should create *desire*. This can be done in several ways: education, work experience, ability to work with others, interest in your field, interest in the company, and responsibilities on previous assignments. Choose your strongest traits, and expand on them in the middle paragraph(s). You may want to reemphasize certain points given in the resume or bring out additional facts not previously covered. It will be easier to bring out facts such as your interest in the company or to give examples of your ability to work with others in this section of the letter than it will be on the resume.

The Closing Paragraph

The closing paragraph calls for action. Just like a sales letter, the last paragraph should "close the sale." After you have built up a desire, you should make it easy for the employer to buy. You should clearly state when you will be available to talk to the employer. Be specific: Give telephone numbers where you can be reached both at work and off work. You could have a tremendous background and sell yourself very well, but if the employer can't reach you, everything could be lost!

Paper and Format

The stationery you use for your cover letter should match your resume. If you plan to use a color other than white, be sure to obtain envelopes to match. The stationery should be a high-quality bond. *Do not* use stationery from the company where you work; your willingness to "borrow" your employer's paper will not speak highly of your ethics. You may wish to use engraved stationery. If you do, be sure that it is business size (8-1/2" x 11") and matches the paper used for the resume. The type face for the cover letter should be identical to that used in the resume. Again, working on a personal computer allows you to store your letters on disk so you can "cut and paste" new names, addresses, and information at will.

Follow the same format rules that you would for a standard business letter. Extreme block style (all parts starting at the left margin) or modified block (heading, closing, and signature line starting at the center or centered) is preferable. Keep side, top, and bottom margins at least one inch. Be sure to spell out all words in a formal business letter.

Preferably address the letter to the person who has the power to hire. If you do not know the name of this person, you may be able to look it up in one of the following standard reference books: *Standard and Poor's Register of Corporations, Directors and Executives, Thomas Register of American Manufacturers, Moody's Industrial Manual, Dun and Bradstreet* or reference books pertaining to your local area. If the letter is to be addressed to a woman address the letter to Ms. If you are answering a "blind ad" from a newspaper, use "Dear Sir or Madam" as the salutation and not "Dear Sir," which immediately excludes at least half of your audience. Type only your name in the signature line. Do not use your present title, because you are not writing the letter on behalf of your present employer.

Omit Salary History

Job ads may ask that you include your salary history or salary requirements with your cover letter. As mentioned earlier, including such information is usually a losing proposition. First, you may not require a salary that exceeds your highest former salary—you may be willing to work for less depending on the job and your current requirements. Thus, including your highest previous or current salary may be misleading to a potential employer and cause you to be unnecessarily eliminated from consideration. Second, you do not want an employer to make you a "low-ball" salary offer based on your previous low salaries. I recommend that you ignore the request and submit your best resume and a powerful cover letter without mentioning salary history. Or, respond to the request with a general statement such as "I am hesitant to mention salary requirements in a letter of this nature, but I will be happy to furnish such information when we speak. My primary goal is to attain a position that will utilize my talents and experience."

Proofread

Have at least one other person read and proofread your cover letter. It is crucial that you eliminate all mistakes in grammar and typos, and only another set of eyes can help you do that.

Keep a Copy

Keep a copy of your letter, and keep a written record as you mail out resumes and letters. That way you can follow up by telephoning for an interview if you do not hear from the addressee within a few days. If you have been turned down for an interview, consider sending thank-you letters anyway, as it will leave a favorable impression on the employer. (Chapter 10 contains a sample thank-you letter.)

**Cover Letter
Format**

820 University Avenue, Apt. N-4
San Diego, California 92103
June 30, 1998

Ms. Karen Kemp, Personnel Manager
Prospect Press
495 West 5th Street
Dubuque, Iowa 52001

*Use complete title
and address;
don't abbreviate.*

Dear Ms. Kemp:

*If possible, address it to
the proper person rather than
"Dear Sir or Madam."*

Opening paragraph: Create ATTENTION
Use one of the following:
    A. Summary opening
    B. Name opening
    C. Request opening
    D. Question opening

Middle paragraph(s): Create DESIRE
Devote to one of these:
    A. Education
    B. Work experience
    C. Ability to work with others
    D. Interest in your field
    E. Interest in the company
    F. Responsibilities on previous assignments

Closing paragraph: Call for ACTION
The last paragraph usually asks for action. You ask for an interview and say you will come to the employer's office when it is convenient. Make action easy by giving your telephone number and hours to call if someone can't answer the telephone throughout the day or evening. You also might say you will call for an interview.

Sincerely,

Georgia A. Batting

Georgia A. Batting

Always sign letters.

Enclosure

*Top and bottom margins
should be equal.*

**Sample Cover
Letter: Person
with a Disability**

169 West Lake Street
Minneapolis, Minnesota 55119
May 18, 1997

Ms. Virginia Cole
Vice President, Personnel Relations
Minnesota Mining & Manufacturing Co.
3M Center
St. Paul, Minnesota 55101

Dear Ms. Cole:

I will complete my bachelor's degree in Accounting in June 1995. I possess a strong desire to become a Certified Public Accountant and have concentrated on the area of auditing.

My diversified background offers experience in the areas of accounts receivable, accounts payable, budgeting, invoicing, purchasing, sales, inventory control, employee management, and public relations. Enclosed is my resume, which further details my work experience.

I want to make you aware that I am paralyzed from the waist down and use a wheelchair. This has posed no problems for me at my other positions. I am able to drive my own car, which is equipped with assistive devices, and I am familiar enough with 3M to know that it is wheelchair-accessible.

I will be calling your office on Wednesday, June 14, to inquire about the possibility of interviewing with you. Please do not hesitate to contact me at (612) 990-9292 if you desire any additional information.

Very truly yours,

Stuart Foster

Stuart Foster

Enclosure

**Sample
Cover Letter**

871 Pasadena Avenue
Irvine, California 02716
January 18, 1998

Mr. Lewis M. Cunningham
Hughes Aircraft Company
Ground Systems Group
Employment Department 10-915-T
P.O. Box 4275
Fullerton, California 92364

Dear Mr. Cunningham:

Can you use someone with experience in negotiating prices . . . selecting supplies . . . capital and construction purchasing?

These are the qualifications you are seeking in a buyer, as was published in the January 15 advertisement in the *Los Angeles Times*. I believe that my experience and education make me the person you are looking for.

For ten years I have experienced all facets of purchasing, from procuring materials to contract negotiating in support of company requirements. The work was enjoyable, as well as educational. I am confident that my experience will help me contribute to the work in your company.

As you will see from the attached resume, my successful purchasing background, along with my interest and education in electronics, provides me with the confidence that I can bring your company the knowledge and responsibility your work demands.

If my qualifications meet your needs, Mr. Cunningham, may I discuss with you the possibility of working for the Hughes Company?

Sincerely yours,

William G. Thompson

William G. Thompson

Enclosure

**Sample Cover
Letter: Response
to an Ad**

1072 Redondo Blvd., #22
Marina del Rey, California 90043
May 14, 1998

Post Office Box 808
Los Angeles Times
Los Angeles, California 90041

Dear Sir or Madam:

This is in response to your advertisement for an Estate Advertising Coordinator, which appeared in the *Los Angeles Times* on Sunday, May 13. As the comparison shows, my experience and background match this position's requirements.

Your Requirements	My Qualifications
• Experience in writing press releases	B.S. Degree in Public Relations
• Mac knowledge with Microsoft Word & Quark	Familiar with Mac (Microsoft & Quark)
• Real estate experience	Three years' experience as real estate salesperson

As additional information, enclosed is a copy of my resume. I would like an opportunity to personally discuss the position with you. I'll plan on calling you within the next week to arrange an appointment. Thank you for your consideration.

Sincerely,

Katie G. Brecht

Katie G. Brecht

Enclosure

Sample Cover Letter Using a Request Opening (Seeking Career Advancement)

224 Warren Road
Detroit, Michigan 48207
November 2, 1998

Mr. Donald Jarvis
Vice President, Marketing
Kellogg Company
235 Porter Street
Battle Creek, Michigan 49016

Dear Mr. Jarvis:

I would like to be considered for a position as an assistant in one of your marketing departments at Kellogg Company in areas of advertising, sales promotion, marketing research, or brand management.

Highlights of my achievements that qualify me for an assistant position in marketing are: generated marked increase in sales and expansion of business with astute advertising program for fledgling microcomputer development company; directed state of Michigan's most successful used book sale for a national educational organization; and wrote a number of successful, locally performed drama skits.

With my initial home economics training, which includes technical and science courses, I have been strongly product- and sales-oriented in my multifaceted, broad-based experiences in and out of the home. I work well in groups, managing and being managed with about equal agility.

I am interested in interviewing with you or one of your associates. I can be reached most days and evenings at my home residence phone number, (313) 663-9101, to arrange for an interview at a mutually convenient time.

In closing, it was a pleasure to read in *Marketing News* of your recent promotion to Vice President of Marketing at Kellogg Company, and I would like to offer my congratulations.

With best regards,

Janet L. Pearlman

Janet L. Pearlman

Enclosure

Sample Cover Letter Using a Summary Opening (Transition)

1101 Sherman Way #201
Sherman Oaks, California 91413
(213) 642-9812
April 15, 1998

Personnel Services
Los Angeles Pierce College
6201 Winnetka Avenue
Woodland Hills, California 91371

Sir or Madam:

I would like to apply for the position of Dean of Admissions and Records at Los Angeles Pierce College. I am enclosing my Vitae for your consideration.

As my Vitae indicates, I have gained broad experience in the admission and records processes and procedures through daily student contact and semester registration periods.

My special skills that are relevant to this position include interpretation of policies for students regarding graduation, general education certification, credit by examination, vocational certification, and military credit. I also have working knowledge of foreign student residence requirements and their appropriate permits. I have acquired working knowledge of the legal provisions related to student admission, attendance, and record keeping.

I am looking forward to meeting your selection committee so that I may have the opportunity to discuss with you my qualifications for the position of Dean of Admissions and Records.

Sincerely,

Ruth M. Sanchez

Ruth M. Sanchez

Enclosure

Sample Cover Letter Using a Name Opening (Transition)

7351 East 42nd Street
Indianapolis, Indiana 46226
January 4, 1998

Mr. Kenneth Richmond
Leisure and Cultural Services
City of Fort Lauderdale
201 Coral Circle
Fort Lauderdale, Florida 33903

Dear Mr. Richmond:

Susan Trity suggested I contact you concerning the Therapeutic Recreation Supervisor position available with the City of Fort Lauderdale. I have worked with the City of Indianapolis Therapeutic Recreation Program for three years. Currently I am Director of the School Year Program and the Adult Evening Program. I am confident my experience with Indianapolis qualifies me for this supervisor position.

While with the Indianapolis Therapeutic Program I had the responsibilities of program planning, assessment and evaluation, as well as staff and participant assessments and evaluations. My experience includes working with Educable Mentally Retarded, Trainable Mentally Retarded, Autistic, Aphasic, and Developmentally Disabled. During the summer program I was Director of the Special Youngsters and assisted with the TMR Teens. I have been involved with Special Olympics and fund-raising projects. The enclosed resume will give you more information concerning my work experience and education.

Please feel free to contact me at my home, (317) 772-8080, or at Greenwood Recreation Center, (317) 772-9000. I would be glad to meet with you at your convenience to discuss my working with the City of Fort Lauderdale's Therapeutic Recreation Program.

Sincerely,

Debra Donaldson

Debra Donaldson

Enclosure

**Sample Cover
Letter Using
Request Opening
(Entry Level)**

Janet Cushman
8808 Mockingbird Lane
Dallas, Texas 75205
May 24, 1998

Delta Airlines
Atlanta International Airport
Atlanta, Georgia 30306

Sir or Madam:

Please accept this letter as an expression of interest in the position of Flight Attendant.

I have enclosed a copy of my resume for your review. I am familiar with the requirements for success in the Flight Attendant profession and believe I possess the right combination of public-contact experience and interpersonal skills.

My current full-time position in a health spa has provided the opportunity to work in a high-pressure, team environment, where it is essential to be able to work closely with my colleagues in order to complete assignments.

I am seeking a career that will allow me to apply my interpersonal skills to the fullest and pursue my commitment to serving the public. I believe that the Flight Attendant profession provides the best possible avenue along which to achieve these goals, and that, in turn, I am able to become a real asset to your company as a member of your passenger service team.

Thank you for your time and consideration. I would welcome a personal interview in which we may discuss my potential contributions to your company. Please telephone me at (214) 669-2201 after 2:00 p.m. and suggest a time at which it will be convenient for us to talk. I look forward to your reply.

Sincerely,

Janet Cushman

Janet Cushman

Enclosure

10 FOLLOWING UP

CORRESPONDENCE

One way to leave a lasting impression is to be innovative—do something different. This is a premise for follow-up letters and thank-you notes in a job-seeking campaign. It is suggested that you send a follow-up letter if you have not received any response to your resume and cover letter after two to three weeks. Chances are that the employer still has the resume and letter on file, so you need not repeat all the information contained in your cover letter. You just want to refresh the recipient's memory and perhaps highlight the qualifications you already stated. You may even have thought of some additional information that could be valuable.

Writing a letter is better than telephoning. You don't want to take someone's valuable time in a business day, but you do want to give the potential employer something tangible to refer to later. (A sample follow-up letter is given later in this chapter.) Also, be sure to send a thank-you letter after each interview. Even if you did not get the position, you are getting your name out in the open so the next time a position opens up, the chances of your being remembered are greater. Again, it is better to write a letter than it is to telephone. (A sample thank-you letter is presented later in the chapter.)

RECORDS

As you correspond with prospective employers, record each contact on a 3" x 5" card. A written record of the transaction might look like this:

Company _Holcomb Hathaway, Publishers_

Contact person _Ann Kelly_

Resume left as calling card _____

Resume and cover letter sent _5/4/98_

Interview _____

Follow-up and comments _Call week of 5/11 to followup._

_____

You can also keep records on your home computer using contact management or personal information manager (PIM) software. These programs are simple to use—they often have a familiar notebook-style interface—and help you keep track of important dates and contracts, while reducing desk paper pile-up. PIMs for Windows include Lotus Organizer and Sidekick 95; for Macintosh, check out Now Up-to-Date or Claris Organizer. These programs are designed for everyone from casual users to high-powered salespeople, so be sure to pick the one that best suits your needs.

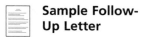

Sample Follow-Up Letter

802 Mockingbird Lane
Dallas, Texas 75205
June 15, 1998

Mr. Ernest Douglas
A-1 Auto Parts
4800 Rosedale Avenue
Fort Worth, Texas 76105

Dear Mr. Douglas:

Perhaps you will remember I sent you my resume for the management trainee position you had open. I am particularly interested in working for your company because of the many opportunities for advancement. I also feel I have the qualifications you are looking for.

You may recall that I have demonstrated my technical abilities in several areas of automotive repair work, and have experienced personal growth from managing two service departments.

I hope that you can use a person with my background. I look forward to hearing from you.

Sincerely,

Gregory G. Hawkins

Gregory G. Hawkins

Sample Thank-You Letter Following Interview

9801 Dallas Drive
Lakewood, Colorado 80742
May 4, 1998

Ms. Michelle Daimler, District Sales Manager
Southern Pacific Air Freight
5340 Arbor Vitae Street
Denver, Colorado 80102

Dear Ms. Daimler:

Thank you, Ms. Daimler, for the time and courtesy you showed me during our interview last Thursday afternoon. As a result of our interview, I'm even more convinced that the position of sales representative with Southern Pacific Freight is exactly the challenge I'm seeking.

In consideration of my fifteen years of sales/marketing experience, interest, and enthusiasm, I feel that I am capable of making a real contribution to the continued growth and profit picture of Southern Pacific Air Freight.

You had mentioned that the next step would be to have another interview with one of your executives. I'm looking forward to that interview, and I will be available at your convenience. Enclosed is my complete employment application.

Sincerely,

Wallace L. Hanks

Wallace L. Hanks

Enclosure

11 THE INTERVIEW

TYPES OF INTERVIEWS

Not every interview is the kind at which an employer will decide whether you are the person he or she wants to fill an open position. There are at least three distinct kinds of interviews. First, job seekers may use *information gathering interviews*, as covered in Chapter 2, to find out information about companies of interest. A second kind of interview, the *initial employment interview*, or screening interview, is used to determine the general eligibility of any given applicant for the position offered. In this interview the employer is looking over a number of potential employees. Your resume has been the factor that won this interview. The third kind of interview is the one (or several) that follows the initial screening interview.

The employer's time is valuable, and if you obtain the third type of interview, you already have gone some distance toward obtaining the desired position. The focus of this kind of interview, or interviews, is to determine your ability to perform the functions of the specific job, your ability to fit into the company scheme, and your real interest in the position. During these interviews, the applicant is usually reviewed by others with whom he will work—perhaps peers, other department heads, or human resource personnel. At some final point the decision maker will, you hope, inform you that you have been selected as the most appropriate candidate for the position.

THE JOB INTERVIEW

Numerous books have been written on the subject of job interviewing, covering forms of interviews and ways to approach the interview. Whatever is said, these basic issues are of primary importance: How do you show that you have the qualifications for the job, and how do you make a favorable impression on the interviewer? You may have the perfect resume and may have conducted yourself well in an interview and still not get the job. Interviewing is a highly subjective process. It is important to go into the interview knowing full well that you are qualified for the position and with the intention of being yourself. Try not to be too disappointed if you are not picked for the first job for which you interview.

You may have to go through the process several times, just as a salesperson may have to make several calls to get one good prospect. It will be important for you to keep your self-esteem on a high level. Each interview will bring you closer to the employment situation that is right for you. As with most things, your interviewing techniques will be refined with practice. What you can do is make sure that you go into an interview situation adequately prepared.

PREPARING FOR THE INTERVIEW

Informational Preparation

If you have done your homework, you will have researched the company or organization to which you are applying. Libraries have standard reference books such as those listed in Chapter 2. Review all of the information you've gathered about the company.

Psychological Preparation

You should put yourself in the right frame of mind before the interview. In order to feel self-confident, you must believe sincerely that you are the best person for the job. You also must convey to the employer that you believe in yourself and that you have valuable skills and talents useful for the job. Experiencing some nervousness is normal. Being well prepared is your best ally to counteract the nervousness.

Physical Preparation

So much has been written on how to dress for an interview that it hardly seems necessary to devote much space to this topic. First impressions are important, however, because they become lasting impressions. Many times an interviewer's opinion is set as soon as the applicant walks into the room. Don't leave this final step to chance; it could mean the difference between your getting the job or not getting it. This is especially true if a number of highly qualified applicants are being interviewed for the same position, as is the case in today's tight job market.

Dress neatly and conservatively, and avoid fads. While the best attire to wear will depend on the job you are seeking, it is always safest to dress on the conservative side. For example, men should avoid wearing flashy ties, and women should avoid excesses in jewelry and make-up. Make sure the clothes you are wearing are clean and well pressed. Most interviewers assume that new or recent college graduates have limited wardrobes, but neatness and cleanliness can always overcome a limited wardrobe.

TYPICAL INTERVIEW FORMAT

Phase 1: The Opening

The first few minutes of an interview usually are devoted to establishing rapport and opening lines of communication. This opening interchange usually sets the tone of the interview.

Phase 2: Information Exchange

The interviewer then will move from the casual exchange to a more specific level of conversation including some direct questioning about your background and qualifications. Sometimes you are asked to respond to an open-ended question, such as "Tell me about yourself." This part of the interview gives you a chance to answer some "where," "why," and "when" questions about your background. Now is the time to describe some extracurricular activities or work experiences that do not appear on your resume. This is also your chance to elaborate upon your strong points and maximize whatever you have to offer. When doing this, be careful that you do not monopolize the conversation. During this time the interviewer will usually present some information about the organization. Here is your chance to ask questions such as: What type of orientation and training may be a part of the job? What are some of the career paths within the company?

Phase 3: Discussion of Company Openings

Part three begins when the interviewer is satisfied that your skills and interests have been identified and you can see how you fit into the organization. You might want to clarify your job objective at this time. The interviewer's description of company operations and activities might help you remember some questions you had in mind. Wait on questions about salary. Let the interviewer bring up the subject of money and fringe benefits; perhaps they are to be covered in a later interview.

Phase 4: Summing Up Time

If the interviewer is interested in you, he or she probably will be more specific about the job he or she has in mind for you, but sometimes this is difficult to determine. Find out the next step. Will there be another interview? When? How soon can you expect to hear about the outcome of the interview? After the interview, say "Thank you," shake hands, and leave promptly. If requests are made for credentials, samples, transcripts, and so on, be sure to follow up with these as soon as possible.

Phase 5: The Interview Follow-Up

After the interview, write a brief follow-up letter. This letter should serve one or more of the following purposes:

1. To thank the interviewer for the time and courtesy extended to you
2. To let the interviewer know you are still interested in the position
3. To remind the interviewer of the special qualifications you may have for this position
4. To return the application form that the interviewer may have given you to take home to complete
5. To provide any additional data the interviewer requested that you may not have had available at the time of the interview

A sample thank-you letter is included at the end of Chapter 10.

QUESTIONS MOST ASKED DURING AN INTERVIEW

Clear thinking is the hallmark of the prepared employee, and you can significantly improve your chances of thinking clearly in the interview process if you have already carefully thought through answers to those questions that almost always come up during an interview. Many prospective employees do not prepare for these questions, so it will be to your advantage to take the time to carefully review them. Write out answers to the major questions, and go over those answers until you have formulated possible verbal expressions of those thoughts. However, don't rely on exact memorization of your answers, which may fail you at an important moment. Instead, remember several key points or ideas that you wish to cover, and discuss them naturally as they occur to you. You may save yourself a critical tense moment in an important interview by calmly and clearly answering questions such as these before you even go:

1. Tell me about yourself.
2. In what type of position are you most interested?
3. Are you looking for a permanent or a temporary job?
4. Why do you think you would like this particular type of job?
5. What are your career goals?
6. What jobs have you held? How were they obtained, and why did you leave?
7. What do you know about our company?
8. What interests you about our product or service?
9. Do you prefer working with others or by yourself?
10. What would you do if . . . ? (Imagined situations that test a person's knowledge of the job.)
11. What are your ideas on salary?
12. Do you like routine work?
13. What jobs have you enjoyed most? Least? Why?
14. What have you learned from some of the jobs you have held?
15. What kind of boss do you prefer?
16. Are you willing to go where the company sends you?
17. What are your special abilities?
18. What kind of work interests you?
19. Why should we hire you for this job rather than anyone else?
20. What are your long-term career objectives?
21. What are your major strengths? Weaknesses?
22. How would you describe yourself?
23. Why are you looking for a change in employment?
24. Do you intend to further your education?
25. Can you get recommendations from previous employers?

ANSWERING DIFFICULT QUESTIONS

It is quite possible that you will be asked questions that may cause you some stress and anxiety. Do not become defensive. Certain positions require an employee to handle stress and for this reason stress interview techniques are used to evaluate the job candidate. Let us consider a question that can be considered "double-edged":

Why did you leave your last job? If you were laid off, simply state that when the company decided to downsize, a number of people were let go, and you were one of them. If you were fired (assuming it was not for insubordination, nonperformance, or theft), be prepared to discuss it. Most people are fired because of a personality clash with a supervisor, a change in management, or corporate politics. Remember to be totally honest! For example, you might say, "My manager suspected I was looking for a new position and asked me to resign."

UNLAWFUL QUESTIONS

The law is quite clear as to what may and may not be asked during an interview. Each state has fair employment practices laws that forbid employment based on race, color, sex, age, religion, national origin, and ancestry.

The following are examples of unlawful pre-employment inquiries.

- What is your age?
- What is your date of birth?
- Do you have children? How old are they?
- What is your race?
- What church do you attend?
- Are you married, divorced, separated, widowed, or single?
- Have you ever been arrested?
- What sort of military discharge do you have?
- What organizations or clubs do you belong to?
- Do you own or rent your home?
- What does your wife (husband) do?
- Who lives in your household?
- Have your wages ever been attached or garnished?
- What was your maiden name (in interviews with female applicants)?

How to Handle Unlawful Questions

First you must decide if you really want to work for a company that asks questions that are inappropriate and unlawful. One choice is to inform the interviewer that the question is unlawful and that you refuse to answer it. Of course, this probably will not land you the job. Remember, too, that an unlawful question may be the result of ignorance rather than malice. Therefore, another choice is to take a tactful approach that will make the same point. For example:

Do you have children? "Yes, I do have children. I pride myself on the fact that I have perfected a system that allows me to be a good parent as well as a good employee. My family obligations have never interfered with my work performance."

PERSONAL REVIEW

This is a self-help exercise designed to aid you in organizing your thoughts, in preparation for a successful interview. Take some time to write out your answers to the following questions. Be able to describe your skills and talents and how you have employed these skills.

Personal Review

1. How would you describe yourself? (A broad "sizing-up" question.) _____

_____

2. What skills or capabilities have you developed over the past year? (Explain those pertinent to the job objective.) _____

_____

3. How did you obtain your present position? (Does it show initiative on your part?) _____

_____

4. Describe your present duties and responsibilities. (Explain fully, but be concise. Use numbers and amounts of money when applicable.) _____

_____

5. What did you particularly enjoy about working at your last position? (Be sure to bring out the *positive* elements!) _____

_____

6. What did you like least about your last job? (Answer a negative with a positive.) _____

_____

7. What was your greatest accomplishment at your last job? (Be specific but concise.) _____

_____

8. In what way has your present position prepared you for greater responsibility? (How promotable are you?)

_____

_____

9. What are your reasons for leaving your present position? Why did you leave your last job? (Be honest!)

_____

_____

10. How would you describe your most recent supervisor? (Be careful how you phrase the negative traits, if any. Be very general.) _____

_____

11. What do you feel are your strongest abilities, and how would they relate to our company? (Where did you acquire them? What is the evidence that you have them?) _____

_____

_____

12. Are you willing to relocate? _____

_____

13. How much do you know about our department/organization/operation? (What knowledge do you have of this particular company? Do some research for this question.) _____

_____

_____

14. What do you see yourself doing five years from now? (Have you set realistic goals?) _____

_____

_____

15. How would a former/present supervisor describe you? (Be honest!) _____

_____

_____

16. What motivates you to put forth your greatest effort? (This gets at your work ethics.) _____

_____

_____

17. Why should we hire you? (This will indicate how articulate you are.) _____

_____

_____

18. How do you work under pressure? (Give some examples; this gets at your working style.) _____

_____

_____

19. Would you like to tell me anything else about yourself? (Do you have additional information that the interviewer should be aware of? Example: If you are bilingual, mention it.) _____

_____

_____

20. Do you have any questions to ask me? (Be prepared with questions for the interviewer.) _____

_____

_____

INTERVIEW DO'S AND DON'TS

1. DO find out the exact time and place of the interview.
2. DO some research on the company interviewing you.
3. DO be neat in appearance.
4. DO be clear about your job objective.
5. DO bring a copy of your resume and other supporting data.
6. DO give the appearance of energy and self-confidence.
7. DO relax!

1. DON'T chew gum.
2. DON'T smoke.
3. DON'T go on talking and talking.
4. DON'T take a seat until you have been offered one.
5. DON'T bring up the subject of salary.
6. DON'T be afraid to ask questions.
7. DON'T take notes during the interview.
8. DON'T slip into reminiscences about mutual friends or old school or hometown ties. You may divulge information that would be best left unsaid.

SUMMING UP

Congratulations! You have completed the step-by-step process on how to write a successful resume. You have had an opportunity to assess your own skills and state them in a fashion so as to market yourself for your chosen career. Through studying the sample resumes, you have been exposed to a variety of work situations and have gained ideas that helped you with your resume. But you have learned more in these pages than how to write a good resume. You have learned techniques for searching the hidden job market and for making contacts. Also, you have gained information that will assist you in preparing for the interview.

The element that remains is most crucial: It is *you*. How will you use this information and put it to work for you? The only thing that can stand in your way for a successful job search campaign is your attitude. Having a positive attitude about wanting to contribute your skills to a potential employer is one of the best assets you can have. The competition, the lack of jobs, and the economy are things to be faced. It is normal to feel frustrated, let down, and anxious, but to let these feelings take over is to admit defeat. People get jobs in the worst of times and under the most unusual circumstances.

Set your goal and follow a plan. If you are positive, innovative, enthusiastic, courteous, and determined, you will be successful. Many persons stand ready to assist you with your job search campaign; all you have to do is ask.

Finding the right job takes time. The decision you make will be a great one. It is something you will have to live with. Finding a job will be a full-time job for a while, but the time you spend now will be an investment in your future. Doing it right can change your life.

12 | WHAT DO EMPLOYERS WANT?

What do employers want to see in a resume? I asked nine employers from a diverse cross-section of the labor market to give some straightforward criticism of resumes in general.

The panel of experts included the following: career planning and placement directors from two large universities; representatives from two executive search firms and an employment agency; and human resources managers from an aerospace company, a life insurance company, a major hotel, and a large manufacturing corporation.

"DL" is president of an executive search firm specializing in accounting, finance, and data processing.

"MP" is a manager specializing in full-time placement in a personnel company.

"MS" is an employment manager for a major hotel.

"PS" is an employment manager for a major life insurance company.

"PN" is vice president of an executive search firm.

"BB" is director of career planning and placement at a large major university.

"GG" is an employment manager for a large aerospace company.

"JM" is a training development representative with a large aerospace corporation.

"KP" is human resources and salary administration manager for a large manufacturing corporation.

1. *What type of format do you prefer?*

KP: Chronological. I like to see the progressions people have made from job to job.

GG: I like dates and names of the companies listed on the left side and definitely on one page.

PN: The functional resume is the most easy to read. It communicates the most knowledge about their abilities and capabilities to me as an executive search person and ultimately to the firm they are going to be working for.

PS: Chronological. If management cannot determine what you have done on a specific job (i.e. functional), you probably will not get interviewed.

DL: Functional.

MS: I prefer a concise chronological account of a person's career high-lights.

2. *How important is the job objective?*

KP: I want the objective to state what you will do for me. I hate objectives like, "I want a challenging environment where I will progress."

PN: Extremely important! If someone doesn't have an objective, how can you place them in a job?

GG: Very important! Do a little investigation to see what it takes to work in that company. Be sure the company is hiring for what you are looking for.

MP: I like one sentence that introduces you to the employer . . . very clear and realistic. An uncrystallized individual might just use, for example, "Management Trainee."

JM: Since our company is very large, a specific job objective is extremely important in helping us know where to route an applicant's resume.

3. *Do you like a qualifications summary?*

KP: It's helpful for someone with many years of experience, but for a new college graduate it's probably not appropriate.

GG: I like either a qualifications summary or an objective statement. I don't see the need for both.

PN: Yes. One sentence is sufficient. It highlights the important things about the person and why they should be considered for the position they are looking for. It reinforces their objective.

BB: It's O.K. It's subjective and doesn't belong first on the resume.

MS: I prefer highlights of career accomplishments unless the applicant is seeking an entry-level position.

DL: No. Financial people are numbers-oriented. The less they read the better. They go directly to each job and see what the candidates did and when they did it.

4. *Please comment on the grouping of skills in the work experience section.*

KP: It has to be short. Tell me what you accomplished in your job, not your responsibilities.

GG: Yes, I like to see that.

MP: Only if it applies to the job you are applying for.

JM: We prefer that skills be grouped in the work experience section under each job assignment.

DL: This is great if you are applying for a sales position. Bullet points are good.

5. *How do you like to see the employment history listed?*

KP: Most recent on top.

GG: I like to see the dates as well as the name of the company on the left-hand side, maybe slightly indented. If the individual has moved around a bit, it may be best not to elaborate on the duties of each position. Attempt to summarize the duties for all companies the individual has worked for.

MS: Last or current employer first. This is logical since the position applied for generally relates to the current or last position held by the applicant.

JM: List employment in reverse chronological order, providing specific dates with months and years noted.

6. *What about education?*

KP: I'd like to see it after the experience section, unless you're a recent college graduate.

JM: Indicate education in sequential order, including level of degree(s) obtained.

GG: On the top for a recent college graduate, towards the end for someone with work experience.

7. *How do you react to a personal statement at the bottom?*

MP: I'm not sure this is necessary. Are they trying to soften me up? There are other ways to highlight this. Put this in a cover letter.

BB: It's O.K. as long as it is job-related.

DL: Personal interests and hobbies are fine. I know people get interviews because they are runners or chess players, for example.

JM: We are not interested in a personal statement and view it as superfluous. Because of the high volume of resumes received, we appreciate resumes that are concise.

8. *How many pages are permissible in a resume?*

KP: Two pages are fine.

PN: Two pages. Most people cannot confine it to one page after they have been working for some time.

MP: One page only, please.

GG: One page for a recent graduate. Possibly two pages for an experienced person.

JM: We prefer no more than a two-page resume, but it can be accompanied by a longer, more detailed list of work responsibilities/skills if the applicant is applying for a very technical position.

9. *How do you like to see references listed?*

KP: I like references on a separate page. You don't need to write, "References available upon request."

MP: List as "Available Upon Request" or leave it out.

GG: Leave them off the resume. Put them on a separate sheet.

JM: Applicants should attach a separate page for references.

10. *Is there anything else you would like to see on a resume?*

KP: Quantify when you can. Say "saved 15 percent," not "saved a lot of money."

MP: Answer the question "Why should I hire you?"

GG: Military experience could be listed, but keep it brief.

JM: Applicants should include their [security] clearance levels, if applicable.

11. *What complaints do you have about applicants' resumes?*

KP: Personal stuff, pictures on the resume, typos.

DL: Mostly misspellings and not thinking.

PN: No objective. No summary of qualifications. Too much detail in work experience. Salary does not belong on a resume.

GG: Too lengthy. Superfluous information.

MP: Formatted incorrectly. Lack of specificity . . . unclear job objective. Lack of consistency.

12. *What about cover letters?*

KP: They need to be very well written and should answer these questions: How did you find out about the job? Why are you applying? What are your qualifications?

MS: I like cover letters as an introduction only. I do not like clever (or attempts at being clever) cover letters.

JM: A cover letter is recommended only when an applicant is responding to a specific ad we have placed.

DL: Excellent. It gives the candidate a chance to give additional information tailored to the job.

BIBLIOGRAPHY

Bolles, Richard Nelson. *What Color Is Your Parachute?* Berkeley, CA: Ten Speed Press, 1998.

Bridges, William. *Jobshift: How to Prosper in a Workplace Without Jobs.* Reading, MA: Addison-Wesley, 1994.

Jandt, Fred and Nemnich, Mary. *Using the Internet in Your Job Search.* Indianapolis, IN: JIST Works, Inc., 1995.

Kennedy, Joyce L. and Morrow, Thomas J. *Electronic Job Search Revolution.* New York: John Wiley & Sons, 1994.

Krannich, Ronald L. *Careering and Re-Careering for the 1990s: Skills & Strategies for Shaping You.* 3rd ed. Woodbridge, VA: Impact, 1993.

Levering, Robert, and Moskowitz, Milton. *The 100 Best Companies to Work for in America.* New York: Doubleday, 1994.

Malloy, John T. *Dress for Success.* New York: Warner Books, 1991.

Medley, H. Anthony. *Sweaty Palms: The Neglected Art of Being Interviewed.* Belmont, CA: Lifetime Learning Publications, 1993.

Sikula, Lola. *Changing Careers: Steps to Success.* Pacific Grove, CA: Brooks/Cole Publishing, 1994.

Sukiennik, Diane; Bendat, William; and Raufman, Lisa. *The Career Fitness Program: Exercising Your Options.* 5th ed. Upper Saddle River, NJ: Prentice Hall, 1998.